15.95

THE ENCYCLOPEDIA OF PSYCHOACTIVE DRUGS

IN 25 VOLUMES
Each title on a specific drug or drug-related problem

GETTING HELP

THE ENCYCLOPEDIA OF PSYCHOACTIVE DRUGS

GETTING HELP

Treatments for Drug Abuse

SIDNEY SCHNOLL, Ph.D.
Northwestern University Medical School

1986
CHELSEA HOUSE PUBLISHERS
NEW YORK
NEW HAVEN   PHILADELPHIA

SENIOR EDITOR: William P. Hansen
PROJECT EDITOR: Jane Larkin Crain
ASSISTANT EDITOR: Paula Edelson
EDITORIAL COORDINATOR: Karyn Gullen Browne
EDITORIAL STAFF: Jeff Freiert
        Susan Friedman
        Perry Scott King
        Kathleen McDermott
        Alma Rodriguez-Sokol
CAPTIONS: Jeff Freiert
ART COORDINATOR: Carol McDougall
LAYOUT: Victoria Tomaselli
ART ASSISTANT: Noreen M. Lamb
PICTURE RESEARCH: Elizabeth Terhune
        Kay Diaz

COVER: *The Scream,* by Edvard Munch, Art Resource, New York.

First printing

Library of Congress Cataloging in Publication Data
Schnoll, Sidney H.
    Getting help.

    (The Encyclopedia of psychoactive drugs)
    Bibliography: p.
    Includes index.
    Summary: Describes how, when, where, and why people
can seek help for drug abuse problems in such places as
crisis centers, hot lines, self-help groups, and programs
in counseling and behavior therapy.
    1. Drug abuse—Treatment—Juvenile literature.
[1. Drug abuse—Treatment] I. Title. II. Series.
RC564.S325   1986   362.2'938   86-1284
ISBN 0-87754-775-0

Chelsea House Publishers

133 Christopher Street, New York, NY 10014

345 Whitney Avenue, New Haven, CT 05510

5014 West Chester Pike, Edgemont, PA 19028

CONTENTS

Former president Gerald Ford and his wife, Betty, attend a dinner that honored Mrs. Ford for her work in battling drug abuse. In 1978, Mrs. Ford overcame a 14-year dependence on alcohol and tranquilizers.

FOREWORD

In the Mainstream of American Life

The rapid growth of drug use and abuse is one of the most dramatic changes in the fabric of American society in the last 20 years. The United States has the highest level of psychoactive drug use of any industrialized society. It is 10 to 30 times greater than it was 20 years ago.

According to a recent Gallup poll, young people consider drugs the leading problem that they face. One of the legacies of the social upheaval of the 1960s is that psychoactive drugs have become part of the mainstream of American life. Schools, homes, and communities cannot be "drug proofed." There is a demand for drugs—and the supply is plentiful. Social norms have changed and drugs are not only available—they are everywhere.

Almost all drug use begins in the preteen and teenage years. These years are few in the total life cycle, but critical in the maturation process. During these years adolescents face the difficult tasks of discovering their identity, clarifying their sexual roles, asserting their independence, learning to cope with authority, and searching for goals that will give their lives meaning. During this intense period of growth, conflict is inevitable and the temptation to use drugs is great. Drugs are readily available, adolescents are curious and vulnerable, there is peer pressure to experiment, and there is the temptation to escape from conflicts.

No matter what their age or socioeconomic status, no group is immune to the allure and effects of psychoactive drugs. The U.S. Surgeon General's report, "Healthy People," indicates that 30% of all deaths in the United States

9

In 1983, Dr. Mark Gold founded a 24-hour toll-free hotline (800-COCAINE) to provide advice and information for people suffering from either physical or psychological problems related to cocaine abuse.

are premature because of alcohol and tobacco use. However, the most shocking development in this report is that mortality in the age group between 15 and 24 has increased since 1960 despite the fact that death rates for all other age groups have declined in the 20th century. Accidents, suicides, and homicides are the leading cause of death in young people 15 to 24 years of age. In many cases the deaths are directly related to drug use.

THE ENCYCLOPEDIA OF PSYCHOACTIVE DRUGS answers the questions that young people are likely to ask about drugs, as well as those they might not think to ask, but should. Topics include: what it means to be intoxicated; how drugs affect mood; why people take drugs; who takes them; when they take them; and how much they take. They will learn what happens to a drug when it enters the body. They will learn what it means to get "hooked" and how it happens. They will learn how drugs affect their driving, their schoolwork, and those around them—their peers, their family, their friends, and their employers. They will learn what the signs are that indicate that a friend or a family member may have a drug problem and to identify four stages leading from drug use to drug abuse. Myths about drugs are dispelled.

National surveys indicate that students are eager for information about drugs and that they respond to it. Students not only need information about drugs—they want information. How they get it often proves crucial. Providing young people with accurate knowledge about drugs is one of the most critical aspects.

THE ENCYCLOPEDIA OF PSYCHOACTIVE DRUGS synthesizes the wealth of new information in this field and demystifies this complex and important subject. Each volume in the series is written by an expert in the field. Handsomely illustrated, this multi-volume series is geared for teenage readers. Young people will read these books, share them, talk about them, and make more informed decisions because of them.

Miriam Cohen, Ph.D.
Contributing Editor

A yoga class in Holland. Derived from Hindu philosophy, yoga exercises help people attain physical and mental well-being. Yoga is one method of relaxation that can help ease the anxiety and agitation accompanying withdrawal from certain drugs.

INTRODUCTION

The Gift of Wizardry
Use and Abuse

JACK H. MENDELSON, M.D.

NANCY K. MELLO, PH.D.

Alcohol and Drug Abuse Research Center
Harvard Medical School—McLean Hospital

Dorothy to the Wizard:

"I think you are a very bad man," said Dorothy.
"Oh, no, my dear; I'm really a very good man; but I'm a very bad Wizard."

—from THE WIZARD OF OZ

Man is endowed with the gift of wizardry, a talent for discovery and invention. The discovery and invention of substances that change the way we feel and behave are among man's special accomplishments, and like so many other products of our wizardry, these substances have the capacity to harm as well as to help. The substance itself is neutral, an intricate molecular structure. Yet, "too much" can be sickening, even deadly. It is man who decides how each substance is used, and it is man's beliefs and perceptions that give this neutral substance the attributes to heal or destroy.

Consider alcohol—available to all and yet regarded with intense ambivalence from biblical times to the present day. The use of alcoholic beverages dates back to our earliest ancestors. Alcohol use and misuse became associated with the worship of gods and demons. One of the most powerful Greek gods was Dionysus, lord of fruitfulness and god of wine. The Romans adopted Dionysus but changed his name to Bacchus. Festivals and holidays associated with Bacchus celebrated the harvest and the origins of life. Time has blurred the images of the Bacchanalian festival, but the theme of drunkenness as a major part of celebration has survived the pagan gods and remains a familiar part of modern society.

The term "Bacchanalian festival" conveys a more appealing image than "drunken orgy" or "pot party," but whatever the label, some of the celebrants will inevitably start up the "high" escalator to the next plateau. Once there, the de-escalation is difficult for many.

According to reliable estimates, one out of every ten Americans develops a serious alcohol-related problem sometime in his or her lifetime. In addition, automobile accidents caused by drunken drivers claim the lives of tens of thousands every year. Many of the victims are gifted young people, just starting out in adult life. Hospital emergency rooms abound with patients seeking help for alcohol-related injuries.

Who is to blame? Can we blame the many manufacturers who produce such an amazing variety of alcoholic beverages? Should we blame the educators who fail to explain the perils of intoxication, or so exaggerate the dangers of drinking that no one could possibly believe them? Are friends to blame— those peers who urge others to "drink more and faster," or the macho types who stress the importance of being able to "hold your liquor"? Casting blame, however, is hardly constructive, and pointing the finger is a fruitless way to deal with problems. Alcoholism and drug abuse have few culprits but many victims. Accountability begins with each of us, every time we choose to use or to misuse an intoxicating substance.

It is ironic that some of man's earliest medicines, derived from natural plant products, are used today to poison and to intoxicate. Relief from pain and suffering is one of society's many continuing goals. Over 3,000 years ago, the Therapeutic Papyrus of Thebes, one of our earliest written records, gave instructions for the use of opium in the treatment of pain. Opium, in the form of its major derivative, morphine, remains one of the most powerful drugs we have for pain relief. But opium, morphine, and similar compounds, such as heroin, have also been used by many to induce changes in mood and feeling. Another example of man's misuse of a natural substance is the coca leaf, which for centuries was used by the Indians of Peru to reduce fatigue and hunger. Its modern derivative, cocaine, has important medical use as a local anesthetic. Unfortunately, its increasing abuse in the 1980s has reached epidemic proportions.

The purpose of this series is to provide information about the nature and behavioral effects of alcohol and drugs, and the probable consequences of their use. The information presented here (and in other books in this series) is based on many clinical and laboratory studies and observations by people from diverse walks of life.

Over the centuries, novelists, poets, and dramatists have provided us with many insights into the beneficial and problematic aspects of alcohol and drug use. Physicians, lawyers, biologists, psychologists, and social scientists have contributed to a better understanding of the causes and consequences of using these substances. The authors in this series have attempted to gather and condense all the latest information about drug use and abuse. They have also described the sometimes wide gaps in our knowledge and have suggested some new ways to answer many difficult questions.

One such question, for example, is how do alcohol and drug problems get started? And what is the best way to treat them when they do? Not too many years ago, alcoholics and drug abusers were regarded as evil, immoral, or both. It is now recognized that these persons suffer from very complicated diseases involving complex biological, psychological, and social problems. To understand how the disease begins and progresses, it is necessary to understand the nature of the substance, the behavior and genetic makeup of the afflicted person, and the characteristics of the society or culture in which he lives.

The diagram below shows the interaction of these three factors. The arrows indicate that the substance not only affects the user personally, but the society as well. Society influences attitudes towards the substance, which in turn affect its availability. The substance's impact upon the society may support or discourage the use and abuse of that substance.

SUBSTANCE
(ALCOHOL OR DRUG)

PERSON ◄───────► SOCIETY

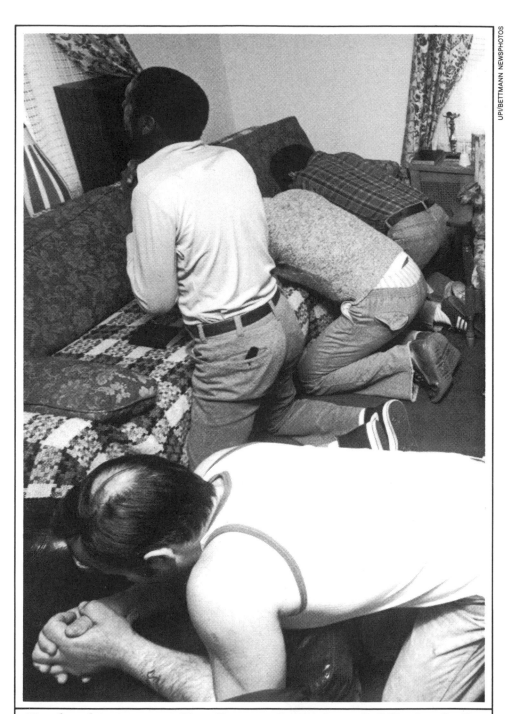

Men kneel in prayer at Pivot House, a Connecticut rehabilitation facility that places a strong emphasis on religion. The name "Pivot" suggests a turning point in the lives of recovering addicts.

Although many of the social environments we live in are very similar, some of the most subtle differences can strongly influence our thinking and behavior. Where we live, go to school and work, whom we discuss things with—all influence our opinions about drug use and misuse. Yet we also share certain commonly accepted beliefs that outweigh any differences in our attitudes. The authors in this series have tried to identify and discuss the central, most crucial issues concerning drug use and misuse.

Regrettably, man's wizardry in developing new substances in medical therapeutics has not always been paralleled by intelligent usage. Although we do know a great deal about the effects of alcohol and drugs, we have yet to learn how to impart that knowledge, especially to young adults.

Does it matter? What harm does it do to smoke a little pot or have a few beers? What is it like to be intoxicated? How long does it last? Will it make me feel really fine? Will it make me sick? What are the risks? These are but a few of the questions answered in this series, which, hopefully, will enable the reader to make wise decisions concerning the crucial issue of drugs.

Information sensibly acted upon can go a long way towards helping everyone develop his or her best self. As one keen and sensitive observer, Dr. Lewis Thomas, has said,

> *There is nothing at all absurd about the human condition. We matter. It seems to me a good guess, hazarded by a good many people who have thought about it, that we may be engaged in the formation of something like a mind for the life of this planet. If this is so, we are still at the most primitive stage, still fumbling with language and thinking, but infinitely capacitated for the future. Looked at this way, it is remarkable that we've come as far as we have in so short a period, really no time at all as geologists measure time. We are the newest, the youngest, and the brightest thing around.*

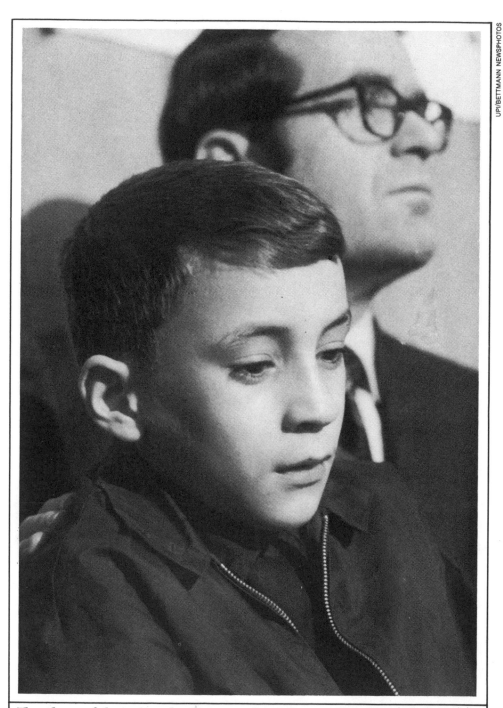

The abuse of drugs is a dangerous and growing problem that affects people of every color, class, and age: this patient at New York City's Odyssey House is an eleven-year-old recovering heroin addict.

CHAPTER 1

DRUG ABUSE

*T*he abuse of alcohol and other drugs is one of the most serious problems facing the United States today. In fact, it may very well be this country's number-one health problem. Many people use alcohol, marijuana, cocaine, and other drugs on a regular basis. Not only does this affect the physical and psychological well-being of the drug users themselves, but it threatens the social and economic stability of the entire country.

Because of the enormous scope of the drug problem, there is no simple solution. Indeed, one might even ask if it is possible to treat drug abuse at all. If the answer is yes, then three additional questions must be considered: Is there one treatment that is effective for everybody? What types of treatment are currently available? In what settings are treatments most effective?

Before these questions are answered, it is necessary to understand that different treatment programs may have widely differing expectations or goals. Most programs follow what is called the *medical model*, whose goal is abstinence from all abusable substances. In contrast to the medical model is the *public health model*, which has as its goal the improvement of the individual's functioning in a variety of areas. This treatment may include the administration of therapeutic drugs that help the person stop self-destructive and/or illegal drug use. Many treatment programs combine aspects of both models and focus on the elimination of harmful drug-abuse patterns and the stabilization of the social environment. These programs reduce family problems and make it easier for the person to return to school or work.

Certain treatments are specific to the drug that is being abused, although others are effective for a wider range of drugs. For example, because intoxication and withdrawal are often different for each drug, only drug-specific treatments are appropriate in these situations. On the other hand, drug-seeking behavior can be treated with more generalized forms of therapy.

Defining the Terms

To understand the nature of drug dependence and its treatment, it is necessary to develop a working vocabulary. Although some of the terms below are frequently used in everyday conversation, the definitions given here are specific to the field of drug abuse.

Addiction is a chronic disorder that is characterized by (1) the compulsive use of a substance or substances that results in physical and/or psychological danger to the individual and (2) the continued use of the substance despite its harmful effects. There are several very important parts of this definition. First, because addiction is a chronic disorder, there is no cure for it. In this way it differs from, let us say, pneumonia, which indeed can be cured. Also, once a person suffers from addiction, he or she must be aware that the problem can resurface at any time. An addict may be symptom-free for a long period and then suddenly suffer a relapse, once again requiring treatment.

The fact that some people continue to use drugs despite their harmful effects reflects the compulsive nature of addiction — it cannot be controlled by willpower alone. The desire to use the drug is so strong that addicts often deny that any problems exist, and thus they gradually allow the drug to become the central part of their behavior. This denial is often the chief obstacle to overcoming a drug problem.

Many physical, psychological, and social problems develop as a result of addiction. Common physical diseases associated with drug addiction include *cirrhosis* (loss of function of the liver cells and increased resistance to flow of blood through the liver) due to dependence on alcohol, and lung cancer or emphysema caused by cigarette smoking. Addiction can also induce symptoms that mimic or even cause psychiatric disorders. For example, the abuse of alcohol and *sedative-hypnotic drugs* (drugs, such as barbiturates, that produce a general depressant effect on the nervous system, resulting in relaxation, sleep, and relief from anxiety) frequently leads to depression. Chronic use of stimulants, such as amphetamine and PCP (phencyclidine, or "angel dust" — a highly dangerous mind-altering drug) can cause manic (excessively excited) or psychotic (mentally disturbed to the point where the victim loses touch with reality) behavior. Not only can drug abuse itself cause negative psychological effects, but withdrawal from many drugs can also produce serious psychological symptoms.

AP/WIDE WORLD PHOTOS

Arresting officers handcuff a suspect following a drug raid in which police confiscated a supply of marijuana. Because marijuana is an illegal substance, anyone who uses it is by law a drug abuser.

Addicts tend to isolate themselves and avoid interacting with others. Families are disrupted and the roles of many family members are forced to adapt to accommodate the addict's changing needs and behavior. For example, the addict's spouse may suddenly have to assume total responsibility for managing the finances and raising the children. Often, family members are so drawn into the addict's act of denial that they too try to cover up the problem. Even employers can fall into this trap. Either unknowingly or in a sincere but misguided attempt to help the addict, employers may contribute to the problem by allowing the employee to be frequently absent or by tolerating decreased work performance.

Dependence is a phenomenon that occurs when a drug is taken during a prolonged period of time. In this situation the body adapts to the presence of the drug. When drug use stops, the body reacts to the absence of the substance, causing withdrawal symptoms. Although dependence is closely associated with addiction, it can occur without addiction (dependence can occur when drugs are prescribed for legitimate medical problems). In addition, the treatment of dependence differs from the treatment of addiction. Dependence is treated by gradually withdrawing the user from the drug; this withdrawal may be successfully completed in a number of days. Addiction, however, generally requires some form of long-term treatment.

Intoxication is a state of changed psychological and bodily motor functioning that is caused by taking a drug. The intoxicating effects of a drug can range from mild sedation and euphoria to coma and death. For most drugs and in most cases of the use of a drug, intoxication is short-lived, because the drug is rapidly metabolized (chemically broken down) and excreted from the body. However, if high doses are ingested or if the drug has a prolonged action within the body, intoxication can last for several days.

Withdrawal is the gradual or rapid reduction in drug consumption until drug use has completely stopped. This process is an essential part of any treatment for dependence.

Each group of drugs has a characteristic set of physical and psychological effects that occurs during withdrawal. This is called the *withdrawal syndrome*. Although the acute or most severe effects gradually subside, usually lasting for several days after drug use has stopped, some mild long-term effects can last for several months.

Detoxification is the metabolism and excretion of drugs from the body, and is the necessary first step in any treatment of addiction. This process can occur through the kidneys, lungs, intestines, or sweat glands. Some drugs, such as cocaine and alcohol, are metabolized rapidly within a few hours. Other, long-acting drugs may take several days to be metabolized; they include *Valium* (a depressant in the benzodiazepine class of drugs) and *methadone* (a synthetic opiate that produces effects similar to morphine and is used to treat pain and heroin addiction). Excretion can also take anywhere from a number of hours to many weeks.

Actor Don Johnson with rock star Frank Zappa on the set of the television series "Miami Vice." Johnson, a recovering alcoholic and former cocaine user, recently participated in an anti-drug television commercial.

Tolerance is an adaptation of the body to the effects of a drug, such that addicts require higher doses of the drug to achieve the effects experienced previously. Although tolerance occurs with most abused drugs, it does not always occur with all of a drug's effects. With barbiturates, for example, while tolerance is developing to the barbiturate's therapeutic — or intended — effects, tolerance is *not* developing to its toxic — or poisonous, and therefore life-threatening — effects. Thus, as the dose must be increased to achieve sedation, the users come closer and closer to ingesting potentially deadly amounts of barbiturates into their systems. In addition, because drug interactions can be *synergistic*, or additive, combining alcohol and sedative-hypnotic drugs increases the possibility of overdose.

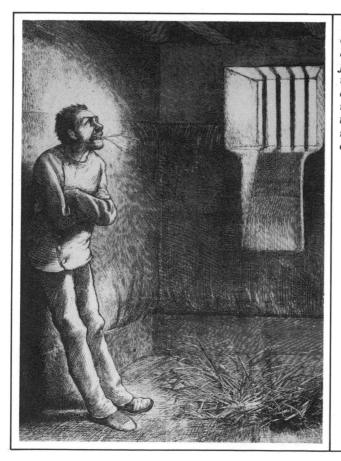

This 19th-century sketch of an imprisoned alcoholic attests to the fact that modern methods of treating drug addiction are much more enlightened than the cruel and inhuman techniques of the past.

THE BETTMANN ARCHIVE

Sobriety for a recovering drug abuser is a state beyond mere abstinence. It involves a reshaping of such a person's lifestyle and values. Because of the complexity of addiction, total "sobriety" is usually achieved only after a long-term treatment process, such as that used by Alcoholics Anonymous, the self-help group for alcoholics. Abstinence without sobriety is not a lasting state, and relapses to drug use frequently follow an attempt at abstinence. Therefore, addicts who are abstinent but have made no real changes in their attitudes or behavior are said to be "dry drunk" or "dry high."

Relapse is the return to substance abuse after a period of sobriety. Relapse is common in addiction since it is a chronic disorder. When relapse occurs, the patient often feels guilty and tries to hide the fact that he or she has been using drugs or alcohol again. This can make it more difficult to treat the patient, especially if the relapse has persisted undetected for a prolonged period of time. Once a relapse has occurred, it is important for the patient to resume treatment as quickly as possible so that gains that have been made are not lost.

A drunk man lies in a New Mexico street. The effects of drug-induced intoxication range from sedation and euphoria to coma and death.

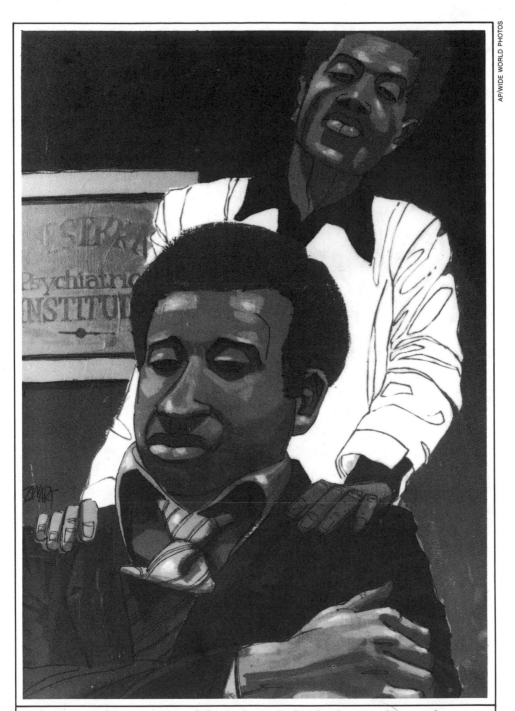

A doctor comforts a victim of drug abuse. Individual counseling and psychotherapy can sometimes help a person to explore emotional problems that often underlie and accompany addiction.

CHAPTER 2

TREATMENT SETTINGS

*T*reatment of addiction can take place in a variety of settings. The required level of treatment should be determined by evaluating the severity of the person's addiction, including the associated physiological and psychological symptoms.

The treatment of addiction is always a long-term process. To receive the best possible care, a patient may need to be involved in different levels of care over the course of treatment. The movement of a patient from one intensity of treatment to another as the need arises is called a *continuum of care*. According to this treatment concept, addicts should enter a treatment program at the level of intensity most appropriate to their needs, and then move through the program progressively. As the addict's status improves, less therapeutic support is necessary. If a relapse occurs, the patient may require a more intense form of treatment. For any program to be most effective, it must allow for the smooth flow of patients from level to level, and it must provide access to all types of clinical services.

Acute-Care Hospital Programs

The most intensive level of treatment takes place within acute-care hospital programs. Often located in major medical centers, these programs are designed to (1) assess the patient's psychological and physical state through observation and the use of diagnostic tests; (2) stabilize the patient's condition; (3) provide a safe, medically approved method of withdrawal from addictive substances; (4) help patients realize the severity of their problem; (5) educate the patient about the nature of addiction; and (6) encourage the patient to continue treatment at other levels of care.

Ideally, treatment will be specific to the needs of each patient. To determine these needs, each person is subjected to a complete examination, including a psychiatric evaluation, a psychosocial-history evaluation (a study of the person's background), an occupational-therapy assessment of the person's ability to live in society, a physical examination (including blood and urine tests), and drug-dependence tests, which measure the extent of the patient's dependence. Acute-care programs are usually equipped to handle addicts who display substantial psychological and/or physical symptoms. Frequently, the origin of these symptoms is not clear and may or may not be related to the substance abuse. Determining the *etiology*, or source of the symptoms, and being equipped either to treat the problem or refer the patient to the appropriate treatment is extremely important.

Acute-care treatment allows a patient to participate in educational-film seminars, family and work assessment conferences, individual and group therapy sessions, and peer-

Residents of a Georgia halfway house gather for a meeting in a local park. Because halfway houses serve as a transition between 24-hour care and independent living, many patients who live in these facilities are able to maintain jobs on the outside.

UPI/BETTMANN NEWSPHOTOS

support group meetings. It must be viewed as a first step in the recovery process, just as treatment in an intensive-care unit needs to be followed by rehabilitation. The typical stay is brief — 3 to 30 days — and the treatment is oriented toward achieving specific recovery goals.

The patient's medical status helps to determine whether acute care will be beneficial. Factors such as psychosis, pregnancy, a history of seizures, or the possibility of a complicated withdrawal all indicate that this form of treatment is appropriate. Contrary to what one might think, withdrawal from hard drugs like heroin does not necessarily require acute care, because such withdrawal is not life threatening. Withdrawal from alcohol or sedative-hypnotic drugs, on the other hand, *can* be life-threatening and therefore often does require close medical supervision.

To provide all the services of acute-care treatment, a high staff-to-patient ratio is necessary. The staff must consist of many highly trained psychiatrists, psychologists, medical doctors, social workers, psychiatric nurses, addiction counselors, and occupational therapists. Because of this requirement and the additional need for sophisticated diagnostic equipment, acute-care programs are extremely costly. Three weeks of treatment can cost as much as $10,000.

Residential Care

Residential care is the next level of treatment. Although it is less intensive than acute care, it gives the patient maximum structure in a 24-hour-a-day program. Most residential programs focus on rehabilitation, which includes education and therapy.

Residential care differs from acute care in other ways. Although the length of stay in a residential-care setting varies, it tends to be longer than a patient's stay in an acute-care program. There are fewer medically trained and psychiatrically trained staff, but more mental health workers and addiction counselors. Also, the daily cost is considerably lower, partially because of the less extensive facilities and the smaller number of expensive diagnostic procedures that are available to the patients.

Individuals benefit from residential care when they are unable to stay drug-free in a less restrictive treatment environment. If a patient has a lack of community support systems (an employer, family, and/or friends) and a history of prior treatment failures, he or she may need residential treatment.

There are several types of residential programs, clearly differentiated from one another by the physical setting, the treatment goals and approaches, and the average length of the patient's stay.

Hospital-based programs are frequently administered in community hospitals, and typically last from three to four weeks. Because hospital-based programs are often the only level of care available in a community, the patient population tends to be quite varied.

These programs focus less on diagnostic procedures and more on treatment than acute-care programs. Although treatment planning is individualized to some extent, the rehabilitation program tends to be standardized — all patients go through a uniform schedule of activities designed for the average person. For many patients, this type of treatment may be enough, but those with complicated cases may not receive adequate attention.

The goal of most hospital-based programs is abstinence, and such programs have strong ties with self-help programs like Alcoholics Anonymous and Narcotics Anonymous. Usually, patients are only given medication during the withdrawal phase of treatment. Family members and close friends are obviously affected by the drug abuser's addiction. When possible, these people — called *codependents* — are actively involved in the abuser's recovery program.

Sometimes, hospital-based programs cater to a specific segment of the population, such as addicted professionals or cocaine abusers. For the most part, these specialty programs differ only slightly from the general programs. What they do provide for patients is a sense that their problem is unique, and thus requires special understanding and treatment.

Freestanding facilities are another type of residential program. Independent of a hospital, they often have a retreat-like atmosphere, with beautiful grounds and recreational facilities. Although their objectives and methods are similar to those of hospital-based programs, freestanding facilities frequently lack important ties with a medical unit. For this reason, individuals with severe physical problems should not go to a freestanding facility for initial treatment.

The length of stay at freestanding facilities is frequently longer than a month, and it is not uncommon for family members to be treated as well. Vocational and educational counseling is often a part of the treatment program. The staff includes a wide variety of professionals, including psychologists, addiction counselors, social workers, and part-time medical personnel. Although they are limited due to a lack of medical services, freestanding facilities have the advantages of providing a positive atmosphere and costing approximately half as much as hospital-based programs.

Therapeutic communities, or *TCs*, first emerged in the 1950s as a means of dealing with hard-core drug addicts, particularly heroin addicts. These communities have a somewhat different therapeutic approach than the other residential programs. One of their major goals is to strip addicts of their defenses and then, when they are most vulnerable, rebuild their personalities and behavior patterns. The staff workers use confrontational techniques with the patients, who live within a highly structured environment governed by strict rules. (Today, TCs tend to be less confrontational than they were in the beginning.) Members support one another and often share in the daily maintenance of the treatment center. In addition, most of the staff are recovering addicts, whose insight into drug abuse makes them effective

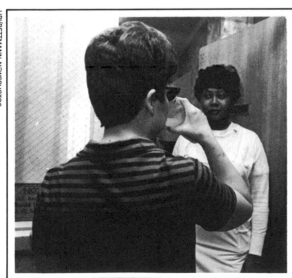

A patient at a treatment clinic drinks a mixture of methadone and orange juice. Methadone, now commonly used to treat heroin addiction, was originally synthesized by German scientists during World War II when supplies of morphine and opium became scarce.

counselors. This community of "workers" helps to create a support system that often substitutes for the family unit.

Therapeutic communities are frequently state and/or federally funded, and thus may be free to all patients.

In therapeutic communities, total abstinence is not always the stated goal. For example, heroin addicts are not always treated for their alcohol-drinking behavior, and so continue to drink. Some therapeutic communities use methadone-maintenance treatment, in which the synthetic opiate replaces heroin. This treatment helps establish relatively normal functioning in the recovering addict and minimizes the intense drug craving associated with withdrawal.

Halfway houses are communal living situations for patients who are at an intermediate stage in their treatment. Most often, halfway houses accept patients who have completed another residential program but continue to need structure to achieve complete recovery. There are also three-quarter-way and quarter-way houses, each one reflecting the degree of structure provided.

Halfway houses are meant to serve as a transition between the 24-hour-a-day program and independent living. Therefore, it is not uncommon for patients to live in these community-based houses while maintaining jobs on the outside. As patients become stronger during their recovery, they move through the halfway-house system until they are finally able to live independently.

Detoxification centers, or *detox units*, provide shelter, clothing, food, and medical advice to needy alcoholics and other drug addicts. Charity organizations such as the Salvation Army often run these free facilities. Since participants usually spend only one night in these centers, and never more than three to five days, complete detoxification is not possible. Detox units exist mainly to provide addicts and alcoholics a place to sober up and to get encouragement to seek more formal, extensive treatment.

Partial Hospitalization Programs

Partial hospitalization programs — also called day hospitals, evening programs, and intensive outpatient services — represent an intermediate level of treatment. Basically, these programs are for those people who do not need 24-hour care but who still need considerable structure and intense support in their efforts to stay off alcohol and drugs. A typical program may run three to four hours per day, five days a week. Treatment does not totally disrupt the patients' lives. They can continue to live at home while working or going to school. Participation requires that patients stay drug-free. This usually rules out admission for people who are suffering from severe drug abuse and need greater structure. Frequently, patients who suffer from medical complications of drug abuse are first admitted to a hospital — where they go through withdrawal and their condition is stabilized — and then enrolled in the partial program.

Similar to residential programs in their approach, partial programs make use of self-help groups, educational films and seminars, and individual, family, and group therapy. Because treatment is given on an outpatient basis, partial programs cost significantly less than residential programs.

Outpatient Services

Outpatient services is a term that applies to any drug-abuse treatment that is provided outside a residential setting. The treatment may range from an informal follow-up to intensive psychotherapy. The quality and quantity of the available services vary tremendously. Some residential programs provide outpatient services in the form of *aftercare*, or "alumni" meetings, at no additional cost. This often consists of regular get-togethers of former patients, whose discussions are led by a staff member. The participants come voluntarily because the meetings are supportive and provide a sense of belonging. The major goal of aftercare is to maintain the patient's abstinence from drugs.

Other outpatient-services programs may include methadone maintenance, educational seminars, vocational and educational counseling, and individual, family, and group therapy. Depending on the staff's professional training, treatment may be primarily addiction counseling (related to the use and effects of drugs and the means by which abstinence can be achieved and maintained) or broad-based psychotherapy. A psychotherapist might address the underlying reasons for drug abuse, always focusing on long-term goals for recovering addicts. For patients who, in addition to their addiction, show significant signs of mental illness, a combination of addiction counseling and psychotherapy helps to sort out the problems so that the appropriate treatment can be provided.

Members of the treatment community do not always agree on whether addicts should or should not receive psychotherapy during the first several years of recovery. Some experts believe that most emotional problems clear up with continued sobriety, without additional psychotherapy.

The types of outpatient services available to drug abusers are endless and include structured (goal-oriented) and unstructured (process-oriented) treatments, long-term and short-term treatments, and general- and specific-issue treatments. Some examples of outpatient groups are long-term psychotherapy groups, relaxation-training groups, early-recovery groups, relapse-prevention groups, recovering-professional groups, and milieu groups (see below), which deal with the immediate environment.

Methadone maintenance programs vary greatly in terms of the type and quality of clinical services they provide. However, all of them have withdrawal and maintenance as their objective. Some programs are merely medication-pickup spots that have modest social goals, such as keeping the heroin addict off the street and out of trouble. Other programs provide a *milieu-treatment experience*, or a time and place for patients to meet each other in a constructive, supportive atmosphere.

Recovering alcoholics and drug addicts work on the Phoenix House farm. Residents of Phoenix House give emotional support to each other and share the chores of maintaining the facility as part of their rehabilitation process.

UPI/BETTMANN NEWSPHOTOS

Some outpatient methadone programs require patients to undergo therapy while receiving methadone, while others provide only therapy. Counseling can range from informal "floor contact," which may take place in a hallway or at the medication counter, to 50-minute psychotherapy sessions.

Medication services are sometimes provided to drug abusers through community mental health centers, which employ medical staff and have at least a modified view of the abstinence theory. Some programs provide outpatient withdrawal to patients who are considered sufficiently reliable and have an adequate support system outside the clinic. Doctors see patients either individually or in groups, during which time medications are prescribed and the patients' responses are monitored. In addition to receiving medication, the patients usually participate in other outpatient programs.

Self-help groups are open free of charge on an ongoing basis to all drug abusers. The 12-step program started by Alcoholics Anonymous came into being in the 1930s when two alcoholics (one of them a physician) realized that the organized health care delivery system was both unwilling and unable to treat alcoholism successfully. They felt that it was necessary for alcoholics to band together to support one another. The program that subsequently emerged consists of a coherent body of well-defined principles and untold numbers of meetings. Today, Alcoholics Anonymous exists in many nations around the world.

In the United States, there are many different types of self-help groups. Their main advantage lies in their availability and universality, and in the strong conviction and dedication of their members.

The programs described above represent the many different types of treatment services available to alcoholics and other drug abusers. Many patients could probably benefit from one or more of these programs. A well-planned course of treatment might include withdrawal in an acute-care setting, long-term care in a therapeutic community or halfway house, and treatment in a freestanding facility. Patients who do not require 24-hour care can participate in partial hospitalization programs or outpatient services. Health care workers on all levels must make sure that patients receive treatment appropriate to their needs, and continually reevaluate the treatment as those needs change.

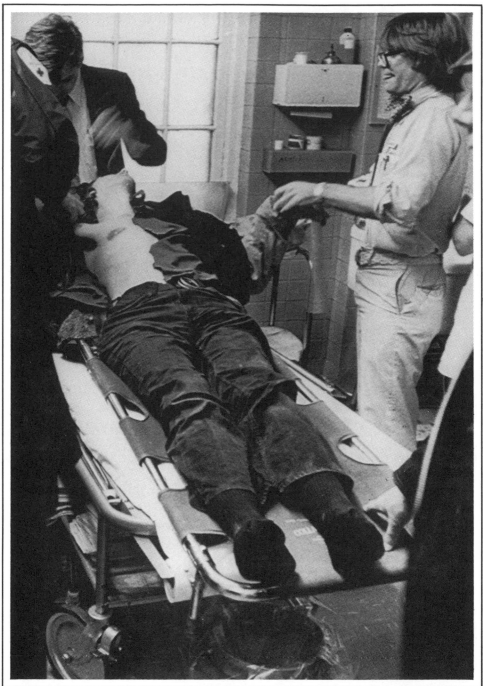

Armed with three guns, this man burst into a Boston clinic and demanded methadone. After taking an overdose of the addiction-treating substance he collapsed. He is shown here being treated at Boston City Hospital.

CHAPTER 3

ACUTE TREATMENT:
INTOXICATION

For most drugs, the effects of intoxication are relatively short-lived. After a drug is taken, the body begins to metabolize it and at the same time excrete it, usually in the urine. Once the drug has been cleared from the body, the effects of intoxication lessen. If a person takes a low dose of any given drug, medical treatment may not be required, and recuperation will be only a matter of waiting until the drug is completely excreted. However, the ingestion of a higher dose may lead to severe medical complications that necessitate immediate treatment. Overdoses, which can lead to a coma or death, require more specific treatment. For some drugs, an *antidote* (a drug that counteracts a poison or its effects) is available. For other drugs, there is no known antidote and treatment must focus on maintaining the drug user's life by assisting respiration and stabilizing the heartbeat and blood pressure until the drug is cleared from the body.

The descriptions of treatments for intoxication with specific drugs are given below. One must realize, however, that street drugs are usually impure. They contain various combinations of drugs and nondrugs; for example, PCP is sometimes added to marijuana. Because each individual drug may require a different treatment, treating an overdose of a street drug can be very complicated.

Opiate Intoxication

Opiates are drugs that are derived from the milky juice of the poppy plant, *Papaver somniferum*. They include opium, morphine, codeine, and their derivatives, such as heroin. These are the drugs for which the most effective treatment is available. The recent development of narcotic antagonists, which work directly on the nervous system, was a major breakthrough in the treatment of opiate intoxication.

The nervous system is made up of a complicated network of nerve cells, which communicate with one another by using electrical impulses. However, between a nerve cell's *axon* (which carries impulses away from the cell body) and an adjacent nerve cell's *dendrite* (which carries impulses toward the cell body), there is a tiny gap called the *synaptic cleft*. Somehow, the impulse, or signal, has to cross the synaptic cleft. This is done by "translating" the signal into a chemical called a *neurotransmitter*, which travels across the gap to specialized areas on the dendrite called *receptor sites*. When enough neurotransmitter molecules become attached to these receptor sites, a new electrical charge is created that

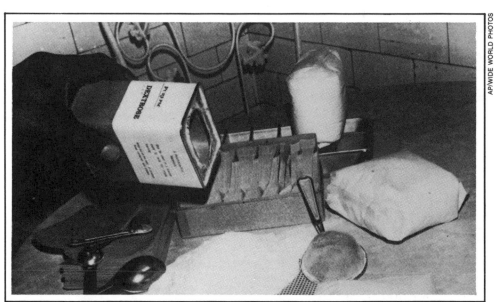

Pure heroin being mixed with dextrose. Dealers often mix drugs with other substances, and the resulting impurity often makes the effects of street drugs dangerously unpredictable and complicates treatment for overdose.

travels down the dendrite to the target organ. The target may be another nerve cell, an organ such as the heart, or a muscle.

The opiates, like many other psychoactive drugs, interfere with the nervous system's transmissions. However, drugs called *narcotic antagonists* are able to block the effects of opiate drugs at the source of their action — the receptor site on the nerve cell. The antagonist competes with the opiate for the receptor sites, removing the opiate from the site and thereby reducing its effect on the body. The narcotic antagonist most widely used to treat opiate intoxication is Narcan (naloxone). Even if a person has severely overdosed on an opiate and gone into a coma, an injection of Narcan will reverse the drug's effects; within a few minutes, the person will act as if there is no opiate in the body.

One of the drawbacks of Narcan is that it is a very short-acting drug, meaning that its effects last only for about an hour and a half. Since an opiate's effects last much longer, Narcan must therefore be injected repeatedly to avoid a relapse into intoxication and coma. This is a minor shortcoming, however, in light of Narcan's overall effectiveness in treating opiate abuse.

AP/WIDE WORLD PHOTOS

This illustration depicts an alcoholic drowning in his own drink while reaching out for help. Severe alcohol intoxication can depress the heart and respiratory system, which in some cases can result in death.

Sedative-Hypnotic Intoxication

The sedative-hypnotic drugs — such as Quaalude, Valium, Seconal, and alcohol — are the substances most frequently associated with acute intoxication and overdose. Unfortunately, there is no specific antagonist or antidote for these drugs. Although alcohol is very rapidly metabolized, some of the other sedative-hypnotics are quite long acting and may remain active in the body for six hours or longer.

In severe cases of sedative-hypnotic intoxication, which is characterized by an impairment of the breathing centers in the brain, the patient may have to be put on a respirator. Special techniques such as *dialysis* (a mechanical process used to maintain kidney function) are necessary if the drug is being metabolized and cleared from the body very slowly, or if it is known that the kidneys are severely damaged, thus reducing the body's ability to eliminate the drug. During dialysis, the patient's blood circulates through a mechanical filtering device that detoxifies the blood and maintains the correct chemical balance in the blood before returning it to the body. Once enough of the drug has been metabolized and excreted from the body by the kidneys, the person can be removed from the life-support systems.

Stimulant Intoxication

Intoxication with stimulant drugs — such as amphetamine and cocaine — can cause hyperactivity (increased or excessive activity) and, in severe cases, seizures that lead to coma. In addition, people who are intoxicated with stimulants can develop paranoia (an irrational fear of being persecuted, watched, or talked about by others) and psychotic behavior. Although there is no specific antagonist for the effects of stimulants, some of the drugs that are used to treat psychoses can be effective in reducing some of the problems associated with stimulant intoxication.

Haldol (haloperidol) is the drug most frequently used to treat stimulant intoxication. It blocks those receptor sites in the brain on which the stimulants act. Although Haldol does not completely reverse the effects of stimulants, some of the symptoms are reduced enough so that the person is no longer in a severely intoxicated state.

Hallucinogenic Intoxication

The consumption of hallucinogens — such as LSD, mescaline, peyote, and psilocybin (the psychoactive ingredient naturally occurring in hallucinogenic mushrooms) — causes a form of intoxication characterized by hallucinations, or sensory impressions that have no basis in reality. This can be very frightening and disorienting, sometimes causing panic, which in turn can lead to physical injury. In severe cases of overdose, seizures may occur.

As with stimulants and sedative-hypnotic drugs, there is no specific drug to block the effects of hallucinogenic intoxication. However, in some cases, Haldol has been shown to reduce some of the symptoms.

The most commonly used treatment for acute intoxication with hallucinogenic drugs is known as the "talk-down" technique. First, the drug user is moved to a quiet setting where there is very little stimulation. Here, someone calmly talks to the patient to reduce the anxiety often associated with this unsettling drug experience. When practiced by a trained or experienced person, this technique can be very effective. Within a short period of time, the intoxicated person, though still under the influence of the drug, is less distressed by its effects. The person is thus able to wait calmly until the drug is cleared from the body.

In April 1975 Karen Ann Quinlan lapsed into a coma after consuming a combination of alcohol and barbiturates and had to be put on a respirator. She was eventually taken off the life-sustaining device and remained alive but comatose until her death in 1985.

Marijuana Intoxication

Although marijuana overdose is rare, users can become so acutely intoxicated that their functioning is severely impaired. In some cases paranoid behavior results. No specific drug is available to treat acute marijuana intoxication; therefore, the most effective treatment is the talk-down technique.

PCP Intoxication

PCP, or phencyclidine, is a chemical compound originally developed for use in clinical medicine. Now, however, it is categorized exclusively as a dangerous drug of abuse. Its acute effects range from mild intoxication, which can include confusion and hallucinations, to severe intoxication, which can include coma and seizures. When the use of PCP leads to severe abnormal behavior (symptoms of acute intoxication include extreme aggression and even temporary insanity), Haldol is effective in reducing the symptoms.

One of the most successful ways to decrease the effects of PCP is to administer medication that makes the drug abuser's urine more acidic, which increases the excretion rate

Leaves from a marijuana plant. Although marijuana overdose seldom occurs, excessive marijuana consumption can lead to feelings of anxiety and paranoia.

of the drug. By aggressively dealing with the removal of PCP from the body, the acute intoxicating effects can be rapidly reduced.

Conclusions

The treatment of acute drug intoxication is best managed by medical professionals who are trained in life-support procedures. At times, drug abusers exhibit symptoms that may or may not be related to the abused substance. Only a trained professional can recognize the differences between drug-related medical problems and unrelated disorders.

There are many "street" myths about how to treat acute intoxication and overdose. These include putting the person in a cold shower, slapping the face, and injecting the person with milk or salt water. These procedures — some merely ineffective, others quite dangerous — only deprive the intoxicated person of appropriate treatment and may even lead to the person's death. If, after taking a drug, someone exhibits strange behavior, or suffers a seizure or loss of consciousness, professional medical help should be sought immediately.

Don't trust that Dust!

The use of PCP (phencyclidine), which is also known as angel dust, can lead to extremely aggressive behavior and even temporary insanity. This advertisement dramatically emphasizes the dangers of the drug.

A patient slumps down in a chair during a group therapy session for heroin addicts. Symptoms of opiate withdrawal include insomnia, nausea, diarrhea, accelerated heartbeat, and muscle cramps.

CHAPTER 4

ACUTE TREATMENT: WITHDRAWAL SYNDROMES

Withdrawal as a phase of drug-abuse treatment can be completed fairly rapidly. Unlike the state of intoxication, which is characterized by the presence of a large amount of a drug in the body, withdrawal symptoms are produced as a drug on which a user has become physically dependent leaves the body. Although it was once thought that withdrawing a person from drugs was sufficient treatment for addiction, today it is known that withdrawal treats physical dependence, not psychological addiction. If drug users are withdrawn from drugs without also having their addiction problems treated, 99% of them relapse within six months. For this reason, withdrawal should always be combined with treatment for addiction.

Withdrawal from a drug usually induces symptoms that are just the opposite of the drug's effects. For example, during withdrawal from a drug that causes sedation, a person will experience agitation and even seizures. Withdrawal from stimulants, on the other hand, can result in depression. Drug abusers typically fear withdrawal. Over the years, however, doctors and researchers have developed procedures that make the withdrawal syndrome relatively mild.

To treat addiction, the patient is first withdrawn from the drugs of abuse. The only time this is not done is when the patient is placed on methadone maintenance and stabilized on a constant dose of medication. There are several general guidelines that are used in establishing withdrawal procedures for various drugs: (1) use a drug that reduces the severity and duration of the withdrawal symptoms; and (2) provide patients with psychological and social support during the withdrawal period so that they do not concentrate on the withdrawal symptoms.

Opiate Withdrawal

Although many people believe that the most severe withdrawal is from opiates, this is not true. In most instances, the withdrawal syndrome is no more severe than a case of the flu. The symptoms of opiate withdrawal include insomnia, yawning, nausea, vomiting, diarrhea, teary eyes, runny nose, muscle cramps, gooseflesh, rapid heartbeat, and slight elevations in blood pressure. Because the gooseflesh resembles the skin of a plucked turkey, rapidly withdrawing from opiates is often called "going cold turkey."

The drug most commonly used to help users withdraw from opiates is methadone. Methadone is a long-acting opiate that can be taken orally. When given in gradually decreasing doses, it eliminates most of the severe withdrawal symptoms. Recently, other drugs, such as Catapres (clonidine), have also been used to treat opiate withdrawal. Clonidine blocks the release of certain neurotransmitters in the central nervous system that cause some of the withdrawal symptoms. The use of this drug in conjunction with methadone has proven to be effective in helping people withdraw from opiates.

Sedative-Hypnotic Withdrawal

In contrast to opiate withdrawal, sedative-hypnotic withdrawal can be life-threatening. Common symptoms include seizures, hallucinations, delirium tremens (or DTs), which are characterized by confusion, disorientation, and the shakes (constant shivering), and marked fluctuations in such vital signs as temperature, heart rate, and blood pressure. If not treated, the DTs lead to death in at least one out of five cases.

Many drugs can be used to treat withdrawal from sedative-hypnotic drugs, among them the minor tranquilizers Valium and Librium. To create a smooth withdrawal, it is necessary to establish the dose of medication that will effectively block the withdrawal symptoms, and then gradually reduce the dose over about 10 days. If this is done properly, patients should not suffer from any of the severe complications described above.

Stimulant Withdrawal

There is no drug therapy available for the treatment of withdrawal from stimulants. When drug use stops, patients who have been abusing stimulants for a long time often experience a prolonged sleep, after which they suffer from withdrawal symptoms such as headaches, nausea, agitation, depression, and sleep problems. In some instances, the depression may be severe enough to warrant medical and/or psychiatric intervention.

Various medications have been tried in an attempt to reduce the problems associated with stimulant withdrawal, but none have proved very effective. A number of medications are currently being studied, though. In most medical centers, treatment of the stimulant withdrawal syndrome simply consists of the staff providing support to the patient.

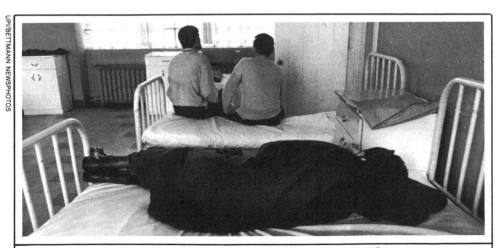

Patients await entrance into a methadone maintenance program. Taken in reduced doses, methadone slowly eliminates opiate withdrawal symptoms.

Marijuana Withdrawal

The withdrawal syndrome associated with marijuana abuse usually consists of headaches, insomnia, and upset stomach. These symptoms are usually quite mild and gradually subside over a period of several days. In fact, depression and a sense of loss may be more difficult to handle than any physiological discomfort. There is no specific medication available for marijuana withdrawal; therefore, in most cases individuals are merely offered supportive treatment.

PCP Withdrawal

Although dependence on PCP has not yet been extensively documented, there is some evidence that withdrawal symptoms occur when a user stops taking the drug. These may include lethargy, depression, increased appetite, and an increased need for sleep. The symptoms usually last from one week to one month, depending on the amount of time needed to clear PCP from the body.

This woodcut depicts a chronic alcoholic suffering from hallucinations and delirium tremens (DT's). One of the principal dangers in alcohol withdrawal, delirium tremens can be fatal if left untreated.

Infants born to mothers taking PCP throughout their pregnancy experience withdrawal symptoms such as irritability, tremors (shakes), and poor appetite, and frequently make high-pitched crying noises. Many of these infants are born prematurely at low birth weights. No specific treatment has yet been developed for PCP withdrawal.

Conclusions

Although specific procedures can be used for certain withdrawal syndromes, the cornerstone of all withdrawal treatments is supportive measures. These include reassurance, drug-education programs, psychotherapy, and peer support. Above all, it is crucial that drug abusers be given help in eliminating the behavior patterns that led to drug use in the first place.

Addicts entering this British rehabilitation center must spend two hours deciding whether they are willing to commit themselves to the program. A patient's sincere desire to quit drugs is vital to a successful recovery.

A former heroin addict at Daytop Village, a drug rehabilitation center in New York, operates a pipe-threading machine. Vocational training can help build self-esteem in ex-addicts and give their lives direction.

CHAPTER 5

LONG-TERM TREATMENT

Recovery from drug abuse is a lifelong undertaking. Although this does not necessarily mean that a person must be in formal treatment forever, it does mean that a successful course of treatment does not end when withdrawal is complete. Too often, people believe that a brief hospital stay accompanied by a withdrawal from the abused substance constitutes a cure. Nothing could be further from the truth. People who have just become drug-free tend to be extremely vulnerable to relapse, and too much self-confidence often leads to treatment failure.

Just what constitutes effective long-term treatment of drug abuse is a topic of continuing dispute. But the methods of treatment discussed in this chapter — chemotherapy, toxicology, counseling and psychotherapy, and self-help groups — must all be considered viable approaches to achieving and maintaining sobriety.

Chemotherapy

In its most general sense, *chemotherapy* is the use of a drug to treat undesirable symptoms or effects. This term is most often associated with the use of chemicals to treat cancer. But it can also mean the administration of chemicals that have specific effects on disease-causing organisms. Chemotherapy can also be described as the use of one drug to treat the effects of another drug.

Using drugs to treat drug abusers involves certain built-in difficulties. For example, it is generally considered inappropriate to treat a person who is dependent on sedative-hypnotic drugs (including alcohol) with other drugs. Prescribing Valium, which is very similar to alcohol in its actions and effects, to an alcoholic who is suffering from anxiety or sleep disturbances is usually not helpful. The newly prescribed drug may just take the place of the original drug, or the person may end up with two dependencies rather than one — a phenomenon known as *cross-dependence*. The particular drugs that may cause difficulties for the drug abuser include sleeping pills and antianxiety medications, such as tranquilizers. Most of these substances have a high likelihood for dependence and addiction, and most produce tolerance.

Methadone maintenance, or the substitution of methadone for other opiates, is an acceptable clinical practice. Although complex theories about the opiate-dependent person's drug hunger and physical need for drugs may be used as justification for prescribing methadone, ultimately meth-

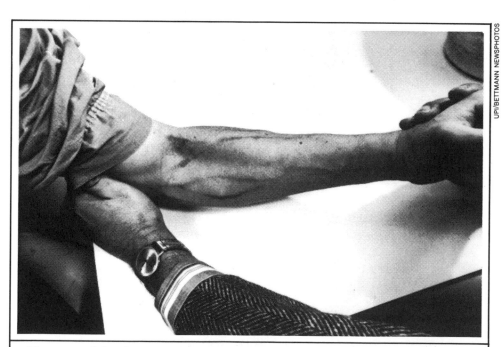

The arm of this heroin addict bears the scars of needle marks. Long-term treatment is usually required for recovery from opiate addiction.

adone maintenance is chosen simply because it works. Many heroin addicts — feared by society and trapped in a self-destructive lifestyle — have been significantly helped by methadone. Often, the introduction of methadone leads to numerous indirect signs of improvement, such as a reduction in overdoses and medical complications (for example, infections, caused by injecting drugs with unclean needles), as well as fewer signs of criminal behavior.

Patients who are on methadone maintenance come to a clinic every day to receive their dose of the drug, as well as to have at least minimal therapeutic contact with a health care worker. The treatment model most often associated with methadone maintenance is the public health model. Rather than promoting absolute abstinence, methadone maintenance has as its goal the minimization of the consequences of drug use. The focus is on the improvement of the drug user's ability to function in the community — to hold a job, stay in school, or remain out of jail. Many methadone clinics do not directly address the opiate-dependent person's other forms of drug abuse. The emphasis is on the abuse of opiates, which is considered to be the primary problem.

Chemical Deterrents

Recently, a narcotic antagonist has become available for the treatment of opiate dependence. This drug, known as Trexan (naltrexone), attaches itself to the opiate receptor sites in the brain and blocks the effects of any opiate that is subsequently ingested. When people who have taken Trexan inject heroin, they do not experience any of its effects. For Trexan therapy to be successful, patients must be strongly motivated to remain drug-free, and they must take the narcotic antagonist in the prescribed manner. If the patient lacks a sincere commitment to sobriety and fails to take the Trexan regularly (usually about three times a week), the effects of the narcotic antagonist will dissipate and the patient will again become intoxicated if any opiates are used.

Trexan is an obvious next step for the patient who has just been withdrawn from methadone, since the pattern of taking medication has already been established. In addition, coming to the clinic to receive Trexan ensures that the patient will continue therapeutic contact. Drug addicts tend to be highly ritualized about their drug use. How, where, and when they get and use their drug is of great importance. If the treatment regimen remains constant following withdrawal, new, more positive rituals can be set up, thus decreasing the patient's anxiety and making the loss of the opiate more tolerable.

Antabuse (disulfiram), a drug whose function is similar to Trexan's, is given to alcoholics while they are sober as a deterrent to drinking. If alcoholics who have been taking Antabuse regularly have an alcoholic drink they experience very unpleasant physical symptoms. These may include headaches, nausea, vomiting, and irregular heartbeat, as well as elevated temperature, pulse, and blood pressure. This negative reaction becomes paired with alcohol in the alcoholic's mind and thus discourages any further drinking. However, depending on the individual's sensitivity to Antabuse and the amount of alcohol consumed, this reaction can be fatal.

Ambivalence about being alcohol-free can have two consequences when Antabuse is used. Either the patient will continue to drink and experience the negative reaction described above, or the patient will discontinue use of Antabuse, and thus will be able to drink alcohol without suffering from the negative symptoms. Therefore, it is important for patients to be highly motivated to maintain their sobriety. In some areas outside the United States, Antabuse is implanted beneath the skin, thus freeing the alcoholic from responsibility for taking the drug. But the implantment approach can make alcoholics feel as helpless in recovery as they did when they were abusing alcohol. Clearly, for withdrawal to be successful, the use of chemical deterrents with alcoholics must go hand in hand with other forms of support therapy.

Psychoactive drugs, or drugs that alter mood and/or behavior, are also used in the treatment of drug abusers. Drug abuse can coexist with major psychiatric disturbances such as *schizophrenia* (a mental disorder characterized by a loss of contact with reality). In these cases, the psychological illness cannot be ignored or separated from the problem of drug abuse, but must be addressed in a comprehensive treatment effort. For example, chronically depressed patients who have used alcohol to alter their moods (and who may actually appear more emotionally distressed once they stop drinking), may benefit from antidepressant medications. These drugs bring the depression under control so that the alcohol becomes less important in the patient's life. The addiction to alcohol can then be dealt with more directly.

It is interesting to note what Alcoholics Anonymous (AA) has to say about the use of psychoactive medication in the treatment of drug abuse. The *Big Book*, the handbook of Alcoholics Anonymous, states that alcoholics should make appropriate use of medical and psychiatric professionals. Nevertheless, members of AA often state emphatically that the use of any psychoactive medication is tantamount to breaking sobriety. What is important to recognize is that this is not AA dogma, but a reflection of the views of *individuals* within the AA community.

Participants in the March on Drugs in 1970 parade up a New York City street. Marchers hoped to direct public attention to the problem of drug abuse, an issue that continues to grow in the 1980s.

Toxicology

Toxicology tests, such as urinalysis and breathalyzer tests, can be useful additions to treatment. When administered on an ongoing basis, these tests (1) provide additional structure for the patient; (2) minimize the possibility that the therapist will remain ignorant of a relapse or continuing drug use; and (3) help in the diagnostic process when a patient's behavior is difficult to explain.

When used as a therapeutic support device or as a mechanism for detecting the presence of drugs, rather than as a diagnostic tool, urinalysis is highly controversial. Some experts believe that this procedure undermines the feeling of trust between patient and therapist. Also, because patients must be observed while collecting their samples to make certain that there is no manipulation or switching of samples, the experience can be humiliating. Furthermore, if an error is made and a patient is falsely accused of using a drug, the therapeutic alliance can be damaged.

Two billboards reflect highly conflicting attitudes towards alcohol in American society. While liquor companies market alcohol as a key to the "good life," treatment programs prove that the opposite is often the case.

It is crucial that the goals of toxicology tests be understood by patients. Treatment personnel also have a responsibility to make certain that the results are as accurate as possible. When toxicology tests are part of the treatment program, the results must be used in therapy sessions. The worst scenario would be one in which the patient is using drugs, and the therapist knows this is occurring and yet fails to confront the patient. In long-term therapy relationships in which the therapist-patient ties are strong, toxicology tests may no longer be necessary. In such cases patients usually tell their counselors if they have relapsed. It is also important to remember that behavior change is the most helpful piece of data available to the therapist. An effective therapist does not wait for the results of toxicology tests before confronting the patient about the obvious behavior changes that so often accompany the resumption of drug or alcohol use.

Counseling and Psychotherapy

Counseling and psychotherapy are often critical to the recovering drug addict's emotional adjustment. It is possible to get sober and stay sober without formal treatment, but for many, going through it alone is a difficult process interrupted by many failures. For some, recovery is impossible without the additional support that the treatment relationship can provide. In general, the more a person does to guarantee adequate supervision and support, the greater the probability of recovery. This means, for example, that although AA may provide the basic structure for an alcoholic's recovery, counseling and the use of Antabuse increases one's chances of success.

A distinction needs to be made between addiction counseling and psychotherapy. *Counseling* is a term used broadly to describe group, family, and one-on-one interventions with the drug abuser. These sessions usually focus on the use of drugs and their effects, and on methods for coping with addiction. Two clear goals of counseling are to educate patients and to connect them with self-help groups. The most frequently used techniques include confrontation, support, and problem-solving approaches. For any therapeutic treatment to be successful, the patient must feel understood.

The people who provide addiction counseling come from a wide range of backgrounds. Some have no formal training but are recovering from an addiction themselves. For them, working with others is often viewed as a final step in their own recovery. Other counselors have both formal and informal training. In recent years, a number of programs have emerged that provide training in addiction counseling.

Psychotherapy not only deals with addiction, but also examines other aspects of a patient's personality and behavior, and studies how these factors relate to the addiction. This approach may include addressing the possible underlying reasons for drug use, identifying self-destructive behavior patterns, and exploring the relationship between patients' emotional states and their drug use. As in counseling, the therapist-patient relationship is a powerful element in the treatment process and is used as a basis for evaluating the patient's ability to relate to others.

Politician Wilbur Mills, television actors Gary Moore and Dick Van Dyke, and former astronaut Edwin "Buzz" Aldrin, all recovered alcoholics, attend a National Council on Alcoholism convention in Washington, D.C. Many people who help others overcome addiction are former addicts themselves.

Although most experts in drug abuse agree that the counseling of addicts is helpful, some deny the importance of the psychotherapeutic approach and argue that it was the failure of psychiatry that brought about the self-help movement in the first place. Other experts see the newly recovering patient as too fragile for an intensive psychotherapy experience and recommend waiting one to two years before starting such treatment. This difference of opinion underscores an important question about the origins of drug abuse: Is it a disease in itself, or a symptom of an underlying emotional disturbance?

It must be stressed that many drug abusers do have multiple problems, all of which need treatment. Thus, the most effective approach is one that is *holistic* — one that addresses all of the patient's medical, emotional, and spiritual problems.

Although drug abuse has often been associated with the rock-and-roll scene, several current pop stars, including Madonna, have expressed strong disapproval of drugs. In a Time *magazine interview, Madonna stated that she did not need drugs to give her confidence and energy; her body produced those feelings naturally.*

There are several ways in which counseling and psychotherapy services can be delivered. These are called *modalities.*

Individual therapy is one of these modalities. Individual sessions, or "one-on-ones," are conducted in private, and allow maximum attention to be paid to specific addiction problems. Counseling and psychotherapy techniques are used during the sessions, which typically last between 30 and 60 minutes. Over time, a relationship develops between counselor and patient that aids therapeutic work. An individualized treatment plan is developed that outlines the objectives of the treatment and the means for achieving them.

Couples counseling and *family therapy* make up another modality. Instead of concentrating on an individual's problems, a therapist deals with the goals of a couple or family. An attempt is made to identify the family problems, to understand how these relate to the drug abuser's behavior, and to intervene strategically to bring about change, and ultimately improve family relations.

First Lady Nancy Reagan, who has campaigned extensively against the national problem of drug abuse, talks with young drug addicts at New York City's Phoenix House, the 24-hour drug-treatment center.

Many times, family treatment must wait until some of the drug abuser's other problems have been addressed. Other times, individual and family treatment can go on at the same time, often with great success. The key is to recognize that the drug abuser's family members also frequently need therapeutic attention. Often, the pain they endured as a result of the addiction was as bad as or worse than that experienced by the addict. After all, the family members lacked the escape that the drugs might have provided for the addict. If family treatment is not possible, however, individual counseling and group therapy are good alternatives for family members.

Group therapy is often cited as the most important modality for providing counseling and psychotherapy services to the recovering addict. When people are addicted to drugs, they become isolated and develop false views of themselves and the world. A group setting can be extremely effective in helping patients see themselves more realistically. It is an environment in which new behaviors can be tried and in which the recovering addict can receive feedback and companionship from others who have had similar experiences. The combination of confrontation and support can be a powerful therapeutic tool.

Additional Therapies

Because addicts have generalized difficulties with work, school, and leisure time, addiction counseling and psychotherapy alone are sometimes not enough to help them function at an efficient level. For this reason, vocational assessment and counseling are often part of a comprehensive treatment. Depending on the age at which the drug abuse began, recovering addicts may or may not be employable even after they are completely withdrawn from the abused substances. Those who become deeply involved in drugs when they are very young often have no marketable skills, and so need to go back to school. Sometimes, a person's career is actually a factor in the development of the addiction. When this is the case, a career change may be necessary. Other people simply need help in learning to cope with the stress and responsibility that come with their jobs.

Treatment for patients in health care facilities often includes some form of recreational therapy. Because substance abusers often began to use drugs as a means of coping with boredom, many of them have little ability to plan ahead, and almost no experience with non-drug-related fun. In the past, most of their leisure time was occupied by drinking or the use of other drugs. Therefore, when these patients become sober, they simply do not know what to do with themselves. Learning to channel tension into productive activities decreases the probability of a return to drugs. Although there is something to be said for a positive addiction (such as an addiction to jogging or weight lifting), it must nevertheless be recognized that even the obsessive involvement in a recreational activity may be a form of escape from emotional issues and problems that should be confronted directly.

Some drug-abuse treatment programs use what may be loosely termed *behavioral therapy*. This approach, which incorporates a vast range of specific techniques, is based on the theory that behavior — whether normal or abnormal — is the result of conditioning and learning, not the result of conscious thought or willpower. One of the most contro-

Synanon is a private rehabilitation facility for recovering drug addicts and alcoholics. Here, members prepare food for distribution to needy families. Helping others is an important part of the recovery process at Synanon.

UPI/BETTMANN NEWSPHOTOS

versial treatment techniques in the field of behavioral therapy is *controlled drinking*, whereby an alcoholic learns to resume drinking in a controlled way, and thus avoids binges. The behaviorists have conducted studies in which alcoholics (many of them highly motivated to continue drinking despite their histories) are given specific strategies for limiting their intake of alcoholic beverages, such as alternating alcoholic drinks with nonalcoholic drinks. The findings of these studies are inconclusive. Although a small percentage of the alcoholics are at least moderately successful in learning to be responsible drinkers, experts do not know why some are successful and some are not. Controlled drinking should not be confused with social drinking or normal drinking. Individuals undergoing the controlled-drinking treatment can never let down their guard when it comes to something as serious as alcoholism.

Aversive conditioning is a behavioral technique that combines negative feedback with a specific undesirable behavior, so that an individual learns to discontinue such be-

Some drug-treatment centers employ unusual strategies in their treatment procedures. For example, the California Center for Living and Learning, which is designed to resemble a Monopoly board, has also adapted the rules of the popular game to create a program to enable its patients to learn the skills needed to cope with the outside world.

havior. This technique has been used in the treatment of alcoholism and other forms of drug addiction. For example, at some clinics both electric shocks and nausea-inducing chemicals have been paired with drinking to help alcoholics stay sober. Some of this rather extreme conditioning has proven effective over a short period of time, but most participants eventually resume drug use once outside the clinic setting.

Another behavioral technique is known as *contingency contracting*, in which the patient signs a contract with the therapist stating the consequences (often the dealing out of a stiff penalty) if there is evidence of a return to addictive behavior. (These consequences vary from patient to patient and are devised in cooperation with the therapist.) This approach is very helpful as long as the contract exists. However, since these contracts have a time limit, patients who are no longer motivated to stay drug-free may simply refuse to renew the contract.

Some behavioral strategies have been very effective in the more traditional treatment of addiction. Techniques such as assertiveness training and relaxation therapy address specific problems that are common to a large segment of the addicted population. However, these techniques are usually part of a larger, comprehensive treatment program.

Self-Help Groups

Self-help groups make up the largest drug addiction treatment network in the world. Alcoholics Anonymous (AA), the parent of all self-help groups, has been successfully helping alcoholics to achieve sobriety for over 50 years. A number of similar groups, most of them founded on the same principles, have emerged since AA was founded. Today, Adult Children of Alcoholics (ACOA), Al-Anon (a self-help group for family members of alcoholics), and Al-Ateen (a self-help group for teenage alcoholics), are available nationwide to alcoholics and their families. The 12-step program on which these groups are based has also been used by other self-help groups to treat other difficult disorders. Such groups include Narcotics Anonymous, Families Anonymous, Cocaine Anonymous, Gamblers Anonymous, and Overeaters Anonymous. All are free and have no attendance requirement.

The 12-step program constitutes a progressive route to sobriety and mental health that is not very different from a well-conceived treatment plan. The steps are worked on in order and at an individualized pace. Participants are encouraged to find sponsors (senior members who have achieved considerable sobriety and are committed to the program) to act as their guides. The first four steps are most relevant to the early phases of the rehabilitation process. Basically, these steps involve acknowledging the severity of the problem, recognizing one's inability to cope alone, asking for help, and making a "fearless and searching moral inventory" of one's assets (positive qualities) and liabilities (negative qualities). The later steps involve making amends to those whom one may have badly wronged as a consequence of drug abuse, and reaching out to help others who are also suffering from an addiction.

AA publishes its own handbook, called the *Big Book*, as well as a great number of additional pieces of literature, from books to pamphlets. Like AA, Narcotics Anonymous and most other such groups also publish booklets that list all the meetings taking place in any given geographical area. Meetings are

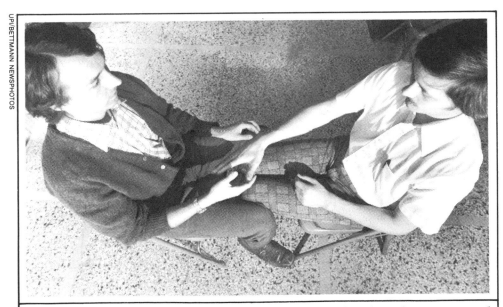

UPI/BETTMANN NEWSPHOTOS

Two men demonstrate a communication exercise used in drug therapy. Mutual trust is vital in helping addicts overcome their feelings of isolation.

designated as "open" or "closed." Open meetings may be attended by anyone. Closed meetings are for addicts only.

There are many different types of meetings. At *speaker meetings*, a member tells his or her story, explaining what life was like as a drug abuser, what was done about the problem, and what condition he or she is presently in. At *discussion meetings*, a topic is introduced, and members share relevant information from their own lives. *Step meetings* focus on one of the 12 steps; members discuss their interpretation of the step and how far they have progressed in their own lives regarding that step.

A recovering addict can function on the fringes of the 12-step program or be totally involved in it. The level of commitment is not specified. There is an emphasis on anonymity, and therefore people typically do not volunteer their last names at the meetings. Nevertheless, addicts do build strong relationships with other members of the group. So-

---

THE TWELVE STEPS

1. We admitted we were powerless over alcohol — that our lives had become unmanageable.
2. Came to believe that a Power greater than ourselves could restore us to sanity.
3. Made a decision to turn our will and our lives over to the care of God *as we understood Him.*
4. Made a searching and fearless moral inventory of ourselves.
5. Admitted to God, to ourselves and to another human being the exact nature of our wrongs.
6. Were entirely ready to have God remove all these defects of character.
7. Humbly asked Him to remove our shortcomings.
8. Made a list of all persons we had harmed, and became willing to make amends to them all.
9. Made direct amends to such people wherever possible, except when to do so would injure them or others.
10. Continued to take personal inventory and when we were wrong promptly admitted it.
11. Sought through prayer and meditation to improve our conscious contact with God *as we understood Him,* praying only for knowledge of His will for us and the power to carry that out.
12. Having had a spiritual awakening as the result of these Steps, we tried to carry this message to others, and to practice these principles in all our affairs.

The 12 steps of Alcoholics Anonymous. Since the founding of this self-help group in the 1930s, millions of suffering alcoholics have achieved sobriety by following the simple but life-saving philosophy embodied in this program.

---

cializing before and after meetings and exchanging phone numbers are informal, though critical, ways of building a support system.

Members come to identify with and genuinely care about other members of the group. When someone is obviously in trouble, the typical response is to reach out. Being involved with 12-step work may include taking someone to a meeting. Sometimes it means sitting up all night with the person or ushering the person into a treatment program. At times, it even means leaving someone alone to *bottom out* — to reach a point of maximum despair and desperation. It is at this point that an addict is most likely to seek and to accept help. To develop the most viable long-term treatment program for any given person, a careful, in-depth assessment must first be made. The intensity and type of treatment needed must be determined. Most often, successful treatment includes the simultaneous use of a number of different approaches.

A young girl answers a call at a drug hotline offering people with drug problems support and advice regarding treatment facilities.

Babies born to opiate-dependent mothers can experience withdrawal symptoms such as rigidity and tremors. Here, a doctor cradles an infant recovering from narcotic withdrawal as the child's mother, a former addict, looks on.

CHAPTER 6

SPECIAL TREATMENT POPULATIONS

*P*regnant women, psychologically disturbed people, patients taking prescription drugs, medical professionals, and athletes belong to groups that present unique difficulties for health care facilities. Drug-abusing individuals within these populations require special treatment for their problems.

Pregnant Addicts

Pregnant addicts pose a unique set of problems. While enduring the difficulties that beset all addicts, they suffer additionally from anxiety and guilt about the well-being of their unborn child.

In general, any drug that affects the mother's brain will also cross the *placenta* (the structure in the uterus that provides nourishment to the fetus) and affect the fetus. So when a pregnant woman uses drugs, she is also delivering these drugs to the fetus. In fact, sometimes the drug concentrations in the fetus are greater than those elsewhere in the mother. One of the greatest tragedies of drug addiction among pregnant women is that their infants are also born addicted.

Recent research into the treatment of pregnant addicts has demonstrated that many of the complications associated with drug use during pregnancy can be reduced. Withdrawing the mother-to-be from drugs, or significantly decreasing the amount of drugs she is taking can, in many instances, eliminate withdrawal symptoms in the newborn infant. Fortunately, many of the drugs of abuse do not cause physical deformities in the fetus. However, behavioral problems are common in the infants of addicts, and in some instances, there is impairment of the infant's mental capabilities.

The use of alcohol during pregnancy can lead to significant problems. This is one of the few cases in which drug use is known to cause physical deformities in the fetus. Fetal alcohol syndrome can cause heart abnormalities, low birth weight, reduced head circumference, wide-set eyes, low-set ears, and a thin upper lip. Mild to moderate mental retardation can also result. At what point in her pregnancy a woman consumes alcohol may be more important than how much alcohol she consumes. If a woman continues to drink throughout her pregnancy, the baby may be born dependent on alcohol, and experience withdrawal syndrome. This often results in the baby crying a great deal, being very irritable, and having problems eating and sleeping. In extreme cases, medication may be needed to treat the newborn addict.

WARNING

DRINKING ALCOHOLIC BEVERAGES DURING PREGNANCY CAN CAUSE BIRTH DEFECTS

NEW YORK CITY DEPARTMENT OF HEALTH
THE CITY COUNCIL Local Law 63

A sign from the New York City Department of Health warns against drinking during pregnancy. Alcohol consumption by pregnant mothers can cause physical deformities in the fetus, as well as heart abnormalities, low birth weight, and possible mild mental retardation.

Babies born to opiate-dependent mothers often have small head circumferences and low birth weights. In addition, the newborn can go through a withdrawal syndrome similar to that experienced by alcohol-dependent infants, but the most characteristic features of the syndrome are rigidity and tremors. Behaviorally, these infants seem unable to respond to parental stimulation. No close relationship between mother and infant ever forms, which in turn often leads to the mother rejecting her baby. To prevent this, the pregnant addict should be taught the skills necessary to cope with the special problems her infant may develop.

Recently, much has been learned about the effects of cocaine on pregnancy. Women who use cocaine during pregnancy have an increased risk of spontaneous abortion (abortion occurring without apparent cause) and premature separation of the placenta. The infants of cocaine-dependent mothers have heart-rate abnormalities at birth and are at increased risk of developing *sudden infant death syndrome*, or SIDS — the completely unexpected and unexplained death of a seemingly healthy infant. They also suffer from withdrawal syndromes for which there are no specific treatments. Although numerous studies have looked at the effects of drugs on the newborn, there is little information about what happens to these infants as they grow up. More research is needed to determine whether children who are born addicted to drugs have significant problems later on in life.

Addicts with Psychological Disorders

For a long time it was believed that patients who were suffering from addiction did not have other psychological problems. Today, however, it is known that addiction can and often does coexist with other psychological problems, and that unless both types of problems are included in the treatment process, the treatment will fail. Before addicts who also suffer from psychological problems can be treated successfully, they must first be gotten off drugs completely. Otherwise, it will be difficult if not impossible for a therapist to distinguish symptoms of psychological disturbance from personality and behavioral disorders caused by drugs. After the patient is withdrawn from drugs and has gone through a stabilization period, a specific psychological diagnosis is made. Appropriate treatment that focuses on both the addiction and the psychological problems may then be started. If treatment includes the use of therapeutic drugs that have a potential for abuse, it is important to monitor the patient quite carefully to make sure he or she is taking medication only as directed.

Unfortunately, there are few treatment programs adequate to the needs of drug addicts who also suffer from psychological problems. Even though there are many such people, they are frequently ill-served by both the mental health care system and the addiction treatment system. Clearly, we must develop more programs to help the drug addict whose problems most often can not be solved by sobriety alone.

Iatrogenic Addicts

Most often, drugs of abuse are thought of as being illegal drugs. It should be recognized, however, that many prescription drugs can be and are abused. In some cases, patients who are being treated by doctors become addicted to the drugs being prescribed for them. In other cases, doctors will prescribe unwisely — perhaps they fail to monitor their patient closely enough, continuing medication past the point where its use is medically warranted. When addiction results from unwise medical practice, it is called *iatrogenic addiction*, iatrogenic meaning any adverse condition induced in a patient by effects of treatment by a physician or surgeon. Patients who are iatrogenically addicted to drugs will often shop around from one physician to another to get enough drugs to maintain their habit. The amount of drugs that the patient may receive from any given doctor may be small, but by visiting a large number of doctors, the patient can collect an enormous amount of drugs.

Iatrogenic addicts are often difficult to treat because they frequently complain of physical ailments that would, on the surface, often require the use of addictive medications. Sometimes these conditions do exist, although sometimes they are psychological in origin. Effective treatment usually means that one doctor has to prescribe and monitor all the medications the patient is taking.

Addicted Health Professionals

Physicians, nurses, pharmacists, dentists, and other health professionals are at high risk for developing an addiction. It is believed that approximately 8% to 10% of all health professionals eventually become addicted. Perhaps these people, who have access to a wide variety of drugs and know a great deal about their effects, mistakenly believe that this knowledge will protect them from addiction. Drug dependence in health professionals can develop quite insidiously.

Addicted physicians and other health care professionals are often driven to steal drugs from their place of work or to write illegal prescriptions to keep themselves supplied. Doctors on drugs are frequently incompetent. This often precipitates malpractice suits in a society already drowning in a sea of litigation. Health professionals with drug abuse problems frequently move around, seeking out new sources of drugs and trying to avoid detection. However, early detection and intervention are the best ways to cut down on the tragic toll taken by this kind of drug abuse.

There are a number of steps that can be taken to treat addicted health professionals. Obviously, one of the first is to limit their access to drugs. This may mean curtailing their involvement in dispensing medication or taking away their

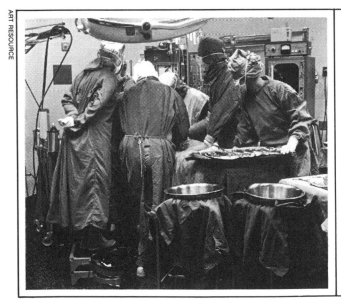

The consequences of drug abuse among physicians are particularly dangerous to society. There are now a number of treatment programs and self-help groups specifically designed to combat drug abuse among health care professionals.

narcotics licenses; sometimes a career change is necessary. Trexan, the long-acting narcotic antagonist, has been shown to be particularly effective for treating this population of addicts. But Trexan only works in treating opiate addiction, and the addict may turn to other types of drugs. The administration of a urinalysis test is one way of assuring that this does not happen.

The psychological treatment of addicted health professionals is somewhat specialized. One of the reasons for this is the intensity of the denial shown by these addicts. They often minimize the severity of the problem and rationalize the reasons for using the drugs. In addition, they frequently express the belief that they are different from other addicts, and therefore do not require treatment. They are extremely frightened of being found out, and so will go to great lengths to cover up their addiction. They also seek to control their treatment and resist getting help from others.

To deal with these problems, specialized treatment programs and self-help groups have emerged. The International Doctors in AA is perhaps the best known of the self-help groups for professionals. It follows the same principles as other 12-step groups and encourages its members to participate in traditional treatment programs.

Police emptying drugs into evidence bags during a raid of a doctor's basement, where he was allegedly manufacturing drugs to sell illegally. According to recent statistics, 8 to 10% of health professionals in the United States become addicts.

AP/WIDE WORLD PHOTOS

Addicted Athletes

The problems of addicted athletes are often similar to those of addicted health professionals. These include intense demands on performance, frequent access to drugs, and a sense of being immune to the problems associated with drug use. Since athletes are in the spotlight, any drug involvement they may have very easily becomes public knowledge. This means that the confidentiality assured most patients is often denied to addicted athletes. The lack of privacy can only compound an addicted athlete's reluctance to acknowledge his or her addiction and seek help.

High school, college, and professional teams have recently developed programs to deal with drug use and abuse. These include educational programs on drugs, urinalysis tests, and the threat of suspension from participation in athletic events. Treatment programs are currently being developed to deal specifically with the needs of the addicted athlete.

UPI/BETTMANN NEWSPHOTOS

Outfielder Willie Wilson (right), who served a prison term in 1984 for cocaine abuse, is now involved in anti-drug efforts aimed at young people.

A recovering addict leaves a hospital rehabilitation program to live on his own. Treatment for drug abuse can be deemed successful only if it creates positive and lasting changes in the patient's life.

CHAPTER 7

TREATMENT OUTCOME

Obviously, the goal of treatment is to have the patient recover from the problems of addiction. However, what exactly recovery constitutes is not so easy to pinpoint. For some people, recovery is simply defined as abstinence. In recent years, however, there has been an effort to expand this definition to include evidence of improvement in other aspects of the person's life — in other words, the achievement of sobriety.

Certainly, stopping the use of alcohol and drugs is central to the recovery process. In assessing treatment outcome it must be determined whether or not the person has continued to use drugs on a regular basis, intermittently, or not at all. Other significant factors of sobriety that must be evaluated include the person's emotional health, vocational adjustment, school performance, legal status, use of leisure time, participation in the community, and role in family relations. Treatment can only be called "successful" if it creates positive, pervasive, and lasting changes in the recovering addict's life. A failure to make necessary changes in lifestyle leads almost inevitably to relapse.

It is very difficult and expensive to study treatment outcome. The difficulties are related to the transient nature of the addict population, complications arising from the fact that data collected on recovering addicts are often supplied by the addicts themselves, and the unwillingness of some patients to cooperate with follow-up studies no matter how well their lives are going. Outcome research also requires verification of information from such sources as schools, employers, family members, and the police. Gaining access to this information is frequently complicated by problems of confidentiality.

In addition to the information gathered from these sources, the medical and psychiatric condition of recovering addicts must be closely monitored. If treatment is truly successful, it leads to better eating habits and improved personal hygiene, regular sleeping patterns, and fewer of the medical complications associated with addiction, such as infections, impaired liver function, and elevated blood pressure. Psychological goals for successful treatment include increased emotional stability, generally appropriate social behavior, and a reduction of psychiatric symptoms, such as depression, anxiety, rage, and paranoia.

Other problems have further plagued treatment outcome studies. The treatment populations are not always comparable. First, the severity of the addiction may not be the same. Those whose addiction is less severe tend to have

David Brink founded New York's Pioneer Marine School, which includes a marine-training program for young recovering drug addicts.

better treatment outcome. However, the concept of severity is not well defined. Second, the presence of other illnesses, both medical and psychiatric, complicates the picture. For example, patients who suffer from depression frequently have a less favorable outcome than those who do not. Third, individuals who abuse a single substance may not be comparable to those who abuse many substances. Members of this latter group may be abstinent from the drug under investigation while they continue to use other drugs.

The measures used to evaluate treatment outcome must reflect the need for assessment in all of the areas mentioned. The most commonly used technique involves surveys conducted at various times following the end of treatment. These can consist of mailings to or personal interviews with subjects and/or family, employers, and friends. Surveys usually do not track a patient's recovery beyond the first two years.

In many instances, the outcome studies locate 50% or less of the population originally treated. When the "find rate" is less than 50%, the study is not considered adequate. Better outcome studies find approximately 80% to 90% of patients.

Actress Mackenzie Phillips and her father, singer John Phillips (center), both recovered cocaine abusers, now speak out against the dangers of drugs.

In well-designed studies, which measure the criteria mentioned above, results suggest that 35% to 40% of the patients are doing well. The best results are usually found within six months to one year after the person has completed treatment. The results tend to show less successful outcome rates over time, leveling out at about a 35% success rate.

In long-term follow-up studies extending beyond one year, the 35% success rate remains fairly constant. However, the patients who are doing well during one time period may not be the same as those who were doing well in a previous period. This relates to the chronic, relapsing nature of addiction. A patient may do well for a period of time and then relapse. This should not be looked at as a complete loss, however. An individual who has been addicted for many years and who then achieves sobriety for even a year or two should be considered a treatment success, despite subsequent relapses. This is especially true if the relapse is of short duration and the person quickly resumes treatment. After further treatment another period of sobriety may follow.

Drug addicts often find themselves on an emotional roller coaster, where euphoric highs alternate with severe depression. Ideally, recovery brings about a stabilization of mood and a reduction in erratic behavior and emotional extremes.

AP/WIDE WORLD PHOTOS

Summary

The treatment of drug and alcohol abuse is multifaceted. *Overdose* and *withdrawal* can usually be treated in a relatively short period of time. In almost all cases, however, full recovery requires that the detoxification period be followed by some form of *long-term therapy*. Many different approaches are used in the treatment of addiction, and all of these approaches have approximately the same degree of success. Much work remains to be done in developing therapies that meet the specific needs of individual addicts. Moreover, the problems associated with getting off drugs and staying off them once addiction has set in remain in many cases stubbornly resistant to all currently available forms of treatment. Many new approaches to treating drug abuse will need to be tried in coming years to overcome this serious national health problem.

ART RESOURCE

Two people jog down a country lane. Learning to fill leisure time, which was formerly devoted to getting high, with healthy activities such as exercise is part of the treatment process for recovering addicts.

APPENDIX

STATE AGENCIES FOR THE PREVENTION AND TREATMENT OF DRUG ABUSE

ALABAMA
Department of Mental Health
Division of Mental Illness and
  Substance Abuse Community
  Programs
200 Interstate Park Drive
P.O. Box 3710
Montgomery, AL 36193
(205) 271-9253

ALASKA
Department of Health and Social
  Services
Office of Alcoholism and Drug
  Abuse
Pouch H-05-F
Juneau, AK 99811
(907) 586-6201

ARIZONA
Department of Health Services
Division of Behavioral Health
  Services
Bureau of Community Services
Alcohol Abuse and Alcoholism
  Section
2500 East Van Buren
Phoenix, AZ 85008
(602) 255-1238

Department of Health Services
Division of Behavioral Health
  Services
Bureau of Community Services
Drug Abuse Section
2500 East Van Buren
Phoenix, AZ 85008
(602) 255-1240

ARKANSAS
Department of Human Services
Office on Alcohol and Drug Abuse
  Prevention
1515 West 7th Avenue
Suite 310
Little Rock, AR 72202
(501) 371-2603

CALIFORNIA
Department of Alcohol and Drug
  Abuse
111 Capitol Mall
Sacramento, CA 95814
(916) 445-1940

COLORADO
Department of Health
Alcohol and Drug Abuse Division
4210 East 11th Avenue
Denver, CO 80220
(303) 320-6137

CONNECTICUT
Alcohol and Drug Abuse
  Commission
999 Asylum Avenue
3rd Floor
Hartford, CT 06105
(203) 566-4145

DELAWARE
Division of Mental Health
Bureau of Alcoholism and Drug
  Abuse
1901 North Dupont Highway
Newcastle, DE 19720
(302) 421-6101

DISTRICT OF COLUMBIA
Department of Human Services
Office of Health Planning and
  Development
601 Indiana Avenue, NW
Suite 500
Washington, D.C. 20004
(202) 724-5641

FLORIDA
Department of Health and
  Rehabilitative Services
Alcoholic Rehabilitation Program
1317 Winewood Boulevard
Room 187A
Tallahassee, FL 32301
(904) 488-0396

Department of Health and
  Rehabilitative Services
Drug Abuse Program
1317 Winewood Boulevard
Building 6, Room 155
Tallahassee, FL 32301
(904) 488-0900

GEORGIA
Department of Human Resources
Division of Mental Health and
  Mental Retardation
Alcohol and Drug Section
618 Ponce De Leon Avenue, NE
Atlanta, GA 30365-2101
(404) 894-4785

HAWAII
Department of Health
Mental Health Division
Alcohol and Drug Abuse Branch
1250 Punch Bowl Street
P.O. Box 3378
Honolulu, HI 96801
(808) 548-4280

IDAHO
Department of Health and Welfare
Bureau of Preventive Medicine
Substance Abuse Section
450 West State
Boise, ID 83720
(208) 334-4368

ILLINOIS
Department of Mental Health and
  Developmental Disabilities
Division of Alcoholism
160 North La Salle Street
Room 1500
Chicago, IL 60601
(312) 793-2907

Illinois Dangerous Drugs
  Commission
300 North State Street
Suite 1500
Chicago, IL 60610
(312) 822-9860

INDIANA
Department of Mental Health
Division of Addiction Services
429 North Pennsylvania Street
Indianapolis, IN 46204
(317) 232-7816

IOWA
Department of Substance Abuse
505 5th Avenue
Insurance Exchange Building
Suite 202
Des Moines, IA 50319
(515) 281-3641

KANSAS
Department of Social Rehabilitation
Alcohol and Drug Abuse Services
2700 West 6th Street
Biddle Building
Topeka, KS 66606
(913) 296-3925

KENTUCKY
Cabinet for Human Resources
Department of Health Services
Substance Abuse Branch
275 East Main Street
Frankfort, KY 40601
(502) 564-2880

LOUISIANA
Department of Health and Human
  Resources
Office of Mental Health and
  Substance Abuse
655 North 5th Street
P.O. Box 4049
Baton Rouge, LA 70821
(504) 342-2565

MAINE
Department of Human Services
Office of Alcoholism and Drug
  Abuse Prevention
Bureau of Rehabilitation
32 Winthrop Street
Augusta, ME 04330
(207) 289-2781

MARYLAND
Alcoholism Control Administration
201 West Preston Street
Fourth Floor
Baltimore, MD 21201
(301) 383-2977

State Health Department
Drug Abuse Administration
201 West Preston Street
Baltimore, MD 21201
(301) 383-3312

MASSACHUSETTS
Department of Public Health
Division of Alcoholism
755 Boylston Street
Sixth Floor
Boston, MA 02116
(617) 727-1960

Department of Public Health
Division of Drug Rehabilitation
600 Washington Street
Boston, MA 02114
(617) 727-8617

MICHIGAN
Department of Public Health
Office of Substance Abuse Services
3500 North Logan Street
P.O. Box 30035
Lansing, MI 48909
(517) 373-8603

MINNESOTA
Department of Public Welfare
Chemical Dependency Program
  Division
Centennial Building
658 Cedar Street
4th Floor
Saint Paul, MN 55155
(612) 296-4614

MISSISSIPPI
Department of Mental Health
Division of Alcohol and Drug Abuse
1102 Robert E. Lee Building
Jackson, MS 39201
(601) 359-1297

MISSOURI
Department of Mental Health
Division of Alcoholism and Drug
  Abuse
2002 Missouri Boulevard
P.O. Box 687
Jefferson City, MO 65102
(314) 751-4942

MONTANA
Department of Institutions
Alcohol and Drug Abuse Division
1539 11th Avenue
Helena, MT 59620
(406) 449-2827

NEBRASKA

Department of Public Institutions
Division of Alcoholism and Drug Abuse
801 West Van Dorn Street
P.O. Box 94728
Lincoln, NB 68509
(402) 471-2851, Ext. 415

NEVADA

Department of Human Resources
Bureau of Alcohol and Drug Abuse
505 East King Street
Carson City, NV 89710
(702) 885-4790

NEW HAMPSHIRE

Department of Health and Welfare
Office of Alcohol and Drug Abuse
    Prevention
Hazen Drive
Health and Welfare Building
Concord, NH 03301
(603) 271-4627

NEW JERSEY

Department of Health
Division of Alcoholism
129 East Hanover Street CN 362
Trenton, NJ 08625
(609) 292-8949

Department of Health
Division of Narcotic and Drug Abuse
    Control
129 East Hanover Street CN 362
Trenton, NJ 08625
(609) 292-8949

NEW MEXICO

Health and Environment Department
Behavioral Services Division
Substance Abuse Bureau
725 Saint Michaels Drive
P.O. Box 968
Santa Fe, NM 87503
(505) 984-0020, Ext. 304

NEW YORK

Division of Alcoholism and Alcohol
    Abuse
194 Washington Avenue
Albany, NY 12210
(518) 474-5417

Division of Substance Abuse
    Services
Executive Park South
Box 8200
Albany, NY 12203
(518) 457-7629

NORTH CAROLINA

Department of Human Resources
Division of Mental Health, Mental
    Retardation and Substance Abuse
    Services
Alcohol and Drug Abuse Services
325 North Salisbury Street
Albemarle Building
Raleigh, NC 27611
(919) 733-4670

NORTH DAKOTA

Department of Human Services
Division of Alcoholism and Drug
    Abuse
State Capitol Building
Bismarck, ND 58505
(701) 224-2767

OHIO

Department of Health
Division of Alcoholism
246 North High Street
P.O. Box 118
Columbus, OH 43216
(614) 466-3543

Department of Mental Health
Bureau of Drug Abuse
65 South Front Street
Columbus, OH 43215
(614) 466-9023

OKLAHOMA
Department of Mental Health
Alcohol and Drug Programs
4545 North Lincoln Boulevard
Suite 100 East Terrace
P.O. Box 53277
Oklahoma City, OK 73152
(405) 521-0044

OREGON
Department of Human Resources
Mental Health Division
Office of Programs for Alcohol and
  Drug Problems
2575 Bittern Street, NE
Salem, OR 97310
(503) 378-2163

PENNSYLVANIA
Department of Health
Office of Drug and Alcohol
  Programs
Commonwealth and Forster Avenues
Health and Welfare Building
P.O. Box 90
Harrisburg, PA 17108
(717) 787-9857

RHODE ISLAND
Department of Mental Health,
  Mental Retardation and Hospitals
Division of Substance Abuse
Substance Abuse Administration
  Building
Cranston, RI 02920
(401) 464-2091

SOUTH CAROLINA
Commission on Alcohol and Drug
  Abuse
3700 Forest Drive
Columbia, SC 29204
(803) 758-2521

SOUTH DAKOTA
Department of Health
Division of Alcohol and Drug Abuse
523 East Capitol, Joe Foss Building
Pierre, SD 57501
(605) 773-4806

TENNESSEE
Department of Mental Health and
  Mental Retardation
Alcohol and Drug Abuse Services
505 Deaderick Street
James K. Polk Building, Fourth Floor
Nashville, TN 37219
(615) 741-1921

TEXAS
Commission on Alcoholism
809 Sam Houston State Office Building
Austin, TX 78701
(512) 475-2577

Department of Community Affairs
Drug Abuse Prevention Division
2015 South Interstate Highway 35
P.O. Box 13166
Austin, TX 78711
(512) 443-4100

UTAH
Department of Social Services
Division of Alcoholism and Drugs
150 West North Temple
Suite 350
P.O. Box 2500
Salt Lake City, UT 84110
(801) 533-6532

VERMONT
Agency of Human Services
Department of Social and
  Rehabilitation Services
Alcohol and Drug Abuse Division
103 South Main Street
Waterbury, VT 05676
(802) 241-2170

VIRGINIA
Department of Mental Health and
  Mental Retardation
Division of Substance Abuse
109 Governor Street
P.O. Box 1797
Richmond, VA 23214
(804) 786-5313

WASHINGTON
Department of Social and Health
  Service
Bureau of Alcohol and Substance
  Abuse
Office Building—44 W
Olympia, WA 98504
(206) 753-5866

WEST VIRGINIA
Department of Health
Office of Behavioral Health Services
Division on Alcoholism and Drug
  Abuse
1800 Washington Street East
Building 3 Room 451
Charleston, WV 25305
(304) 348-2276

WISCONSIN
Department of Health and Social
  Services
Division of Community Services
Bureau of Community Programs
Alcohol and Other Drug Abuse
  Program Office
1 West Wilson Street
P.O. Box 7851
Madison, WI 53707
(608) 266-2717

WYOMING
Alcohol and Drug Abuse Programs
Hathaway Building
Cheyenne, WY 82002
(307) 777-7115, Ext. 7118

GUAM
Mental Health & Substance Abuse
  Agency
P.O. Box 20999
Guam 96921

PUERTO RICO
Department of Addiction Control
  Services
Alcohol Abuse Programs
P.O. Box B-Y Rio Picdras Station
Rio Piedras, PR 00928
(809) 763-5014

Department of Addiction Control
  Services
Drug Abuse Programs
P.O. Box B-Y Rio Piedras Station
Rio Piedras, PR 00928
(809) 764-8140

VIRGIN ISLANDS
Division of Mental Health,
  Alcoholism & Drug Dependency
  Services
P.O. Box 7329
Saint Thomas, Virgin Islands 00801
(809) 774-7265

AMERICAN SAMOA
LBJ Tropical Medical Center
Department of Mental Health Clinic
Pago Pago, American Samoa 96799

TRUST TERRITORIES
Director of Health Services
Office of the High Commissioner
Saipan, Trust Territories 96950

Further Reading

Brecher, Edward M., and the Editors of *Consumer Reports*. *Licit and Illicit Drugs*. Boston: Little, Brown and Company, 1972.

Deschin, Celia. *Teenager in a Drugged Society*. New York: Rosen Press, 1972.

Johnston, L.D., Bachman, J.G., and O'Malley, P.M. *1979 Highlights. Drugs and the Nation's High School Students. Five Year National Trends*. DHHS Publication No. (ADM) 81–930. Washington, D.C.: U.S. Government Printing Office, 1973.

Moser, J. *Problems and Programmes Related to Alcohol and Drug Dependence in 33 Countries*. (Offset Publication No. 6). Geneva: WHO, 1974.

Orford, J. and Edwards, G. *Alcoholism*. Oxford: Institute of Psychiatry, Maudsley Monographs 26, Oxford University Press, 1977.

Glossary

abstinence   voluntary refrainment from the use of alcohol and/or other drugs

addiction   a chronic disorder characterized by compulsive use of one or more substances that results in physical, psychological, or social harm to the individual and continued use of the substance or substances despite this harm

amphetamine   a central nervous system stimulant

analgesic   a drug that produces an insensitivity to pain without loss of consciousness

antibiotic   a drug that destroys or inhibits the growth of microorganisms and that is used to treat infections

antidote   a drug that effectively neutralizes a poison or its effects

aversive conditioning   a technique that pairs negative effects with specific behaviors, such that an individual learns to avoid those behaviors

axon   the part of the neuron along which the nerve impulse travels away from the cell body

behavioral therapy   a therapeutic practice that encompasses a vast array of specific techniques and is based on the theory that normal and abnormal behavior is the result of conditioning and learning, not consciousness or the will

chemotherapy   the use of a drug to treat undesirable symptoms or effects; the administration of chemicals that have specific effects on or are toxic to disease-causing organisms; or, the use of one drug to treat the effects of another drug

cirrhosis   loss of function of the liver cells and increased resistance of blood through the liver; often caused by the chronic use of alcohol

clonidine   a drug used to treat opiate withdrawal that functions by blocking the release of certain neurotransmitters that cause some of the withdrawal symptoms

cocaine   the primary psychoactive ingredient in the coca plant and a behavioral stimulant

contingency contracting   a behavioral therapeutic technique used with drug abusers in which the patient signs a contract with the therapist stating what consequences will occur if there is evidence of a return to addictive behavior

cross-dependence the occasional result of using chemotherapy to treat addiction, whereby the individual becomes dependent on the treatment drug as well as on the original drug of abuse

delirium tremens a condition that includes such symptoms as confusion, disorientation, hallucinations, and intense physiological arousal; it is common to alcohol and sedative-hypnotic withdrawal

dendrite the hairlike structure that protrudes from the neural cell body from which electrical impulses are carried toward the cell body and on which receptor sites are located

detoxification the metabolism and excretion of drugs from the body; or, the process by which an addicted individual is gradually withdrawn from the abused drug, usually under medical supervision and sometimes in conjunction with the use of other drugs

dialysis a medical technique used to aid detoxification when an individual's kidneys are damaged and not functioning properly; involves the use of a mechanical filtering device that takes an individual's blood, purifies it, and then returns it to the body

etiology the causes or sources of a disease or abnormality

heroin a semisynthetic opiate produced by a chemical modification of morphine

iatrogenic addiction an addiction to a prescribed drug, sometimes due to a physician's improper prescribing practices

mania a mental disorder characterized by excessive excitement; or, a type of psychosis with symptoms such as exaltation, hyperactivity, delusions of grandeur, and elevated mood

marijuana the leaves, flowers, buds, and/or branches of the hemp plant, *Cannabis sativa* or *Cannabis indica*, that contain cannabinoids, a group of intoxicating drugs

methadone a synthetic opiate that produces effects similar to morphine; used to treat heroin addiction

morphine the principal psychoactive ingredient in opium, used for its pain-relieving and sedative properties *narcotic antagonist*   drugs used in the treatment of opiate addiction that are able to block the effects of the opiates at the level of their action, i.e., the receptor sites of nerve cells

opiate   any compound from the milky juice of the poppy plant *Papaver somniferum*, including opium, morphine, codeine, and their derivatives, such as heroin

placenta   the structure in the uterus of a pregnant woman that provides nourishment to the fetus

pneumogram   a test that monitors breathing patterrns

psychoactive drug   a drug that alters mood and/or behavior

psychotherapy   a form of treatment that includes an examination of the patient's personality and behavior

sedative   a drug that produces calmness, relaxation, and, at high doses, sleep

sedative-hypnotic drugs   drugs, such as barbiturates, that produce a general depressant effect on the central nervous system, causing relaxation, sleep, and/or relief from anxiety

tolerance   an adaptation of the cells of the body to the effects of a drug, such that the drug user requires higher doses of the drug to achieve the effects he or she experienced previously

withdrawal   the gradual or rapid reduction in drug consumption, such that the drug user ingests consecutively lower doses until drug use has completely ceased

Index

Sidney Schnoll, M.D., Ph.D., is a neurologist and an associate professor of psychiatry and behavioral science and pharmacology at Northwestern University Medical School. He is chief of the Chemical Dependency Program at Memorial—Northwestern's main teaching hospital. Dr. Schnoll received his M.D. from New Jersey College of Medicine and his Ph.D. in pharmacology from Jefferson Medical School in Philadelphia.

Solomon H. Snyder, M.D., is Distinguished Service Professor of Neuroscience, Pharmacology and Psychiatry at The Johns Hopkins University School of Medicine. He has served as president of the Society for Neuroscience and in 1978 received the Albert Lasker Award in Medical Research. He has authored *Uses of Marijuana, Madness and the Brain, The Troubled Mind, Biological Aspects of Mental Disorder,* and edited *Perspective in Neuropharmacology: A Tribute to Julius Axelrod.* Professor Snyder was a research associate with Dr. Axelrod at the National Institutes of Health.

Barry L. Jacobs, Ph.D., is currently a professor in the program of neuroscience at Princeton University. Professor Jacobs is author of *Serotonin Neurotransmission and Behavior* and *Hallucinogens: Neurochemical, Behavioral and Clinical Perspectives.* He has written many journal articles in the field of neuroscience and contributed numerous chapters to books on behavior and brain science. He has been a member of several panels of the National Institute of Mental Health.

Jerome H. Jaffe, M.D., formerly professor of psychiatry at the College of Physicians and Surgeons, Columbia University, has been named recently Director of the Addiction Research Center of the National Institute on Drug Abuse. Dr. Jaffe is also a psychopharmacologist and has conducted research on a wide range of addictive drugs and developed treatment programs for addicts. He has acted as Special Consultant to the President on Narcotics and Dangerous Drugs and was the first director of the White House Special Action Office for Drug Abuse Prevention.